WHALES & DOLPHINS
of the North American Pacific

including Seals & *other Marine Mammals*

Graeme Cresswell, Dylan Walker & Todd Pusser

HARBOUR PUBLISHING

Harbour Publishing
PO Box 219
Madeira Park, BC
Canada V0N 2H0
www.harbourpublishing.com

Edited by Andy Swash (**WILD**Guides Ltd.)
Project managed by Dylan Walker (**WILD**Guides Ltd.)
Cover photo by Lori Mazzuca

Printed in China

Harbour Publishing acknowledges financial support from the Government of Canada through the Book Publishing Industry Development Program and the Canada Council for the Arts, and from the Province of British Columbia through the BC Arts Council and the Book Publishing Tax Credit.

Library and Archives Canada Cataloguing in Publication

Cresswell, Graeme
   Whales and dolphins of the North American Pacific : including seals and other marine mammals / Graeme Cresswell, Dylan Walker and Todd Pusser.

Includes bibliographical references and index.
ISBN 978-1-55017-409-0

   1. Whales—Pacific Coast (North America). 2. Dolphins—Pacific Coast (North America). 3. Marine mammals—Pacific Coast (North America). I. Walker, Dylan II. Pusser, Todd III. Title.

QL713.35.C742007   599.509164'3   C2007-900093-2

THE CANADA COUNCIL | LE CONSEIL DES ARTS
FOR THE ARTS | DU CANADA
SINCE 1957 | DEPUIS 1957

BRITISH
COLUMBIA
ARTS COUNCIL
Supported by the Province of British Columbia

Contents

Foreword

As a young boy, I spent countless hours with my illustrated guide to the mammals of the world, imagining in great detail how I would encounter many of the charismatic animals in the photos. One day I would safari in Africa and see majestic elephants, stalk the jaguar in the jungles of South America and watch brown bear cubs playing in the mountains of Europe. But I always skipped the section on whales. Whales were too elusive and their habitats were too remote. I couldn't really imagine ever seeing a whale.

Soon after I moved to Southern California in the early 1980s, the words WHALE-WATCHING caught my eye in a small ad in a local newspaper. I was incredulous. One could actually go out and see a whale?

I remember that trip as if it were yesterday. A storm front was just on its way out. While still in the harbor, the captain maneuvered the boat close to an orange navigational buoy on which a group of chocolate brown California Sea Lions had hauled out. If the trip had ended after that encounter, I would have gone home happy. But just under an hour later, we found a pair of Gray Whales making their way north through the foam-topped breakers. We followed them for as long as we could, watching them push the tops of their heads out of the water to exhale, before rolling forward and thrusting their majestic flukes out of the water to signal a deeper dive. Finally, on our way back, we came across a pod of several hundred Long-beaked Common Dolphins, just as the battle of the late afternoon sun and the lingering storm clouds produced a magnificent rainbow.

That magical day led me to take hundreds more trips, each just as unforgettable and spectacular in one way or another. I soon realized that whales and dolphins possess many attributes that make them ideal candidates for observation. They are beautiful, powerful, diverse, graceful and distinctive. Even while watching the same species of cetacean there are always new behaviors and interactions to surprise the observer. These trips also showed me that whales and dolphins bring out something special in humans. Their intelligence and social bonds suggest a strong kinship, yet they inhabit a world that is as different from ours as we can imagine.

And so watching whales turned me into a dedicated worker for the conservation of marine mammals, the marine environment and the planet, through the American Cetacean Society (ACS). ACS is the oldest marine mammal conservation organization in the world, operating since 1967. Whale-watching has played a pivotal role in its approach to conservation. It had its first official whale-watching trip a week after being founded, and still offers many outstanding excursions annually to destinations throughout the North American Pacific. We encourage people to encounter these charismatic creatures, an experience which we hope will influence them as voters, citizens and consumers. In some cases, like my own, it can even compel people to pursue an active role in marine conservation.

This guide is the best possible tool to aid field identification for both a novice and a veteran whale-watcher. It uses state-of-the-art technology to combine a wide variety of excellent photos on plates that clearly show the different ways in which each species might show itself to an observer, accompanied with detailed and up-to-date information. But its use extends well beyond that of a "typical" field guide. It is the perfect gift for someone who hasn't even begun considering a whale-watching trip, with accounts of days on the water that are sure to be an inspiration. It also covers all practical aspects of planning a successful whale-watching excursion, and after the trip is over, this book will serve as a valuable reference on marine mammals and their environment.

Whales and Dolphins of the North American Pacific therefore belongs in every wheelhouse, whether it be a vessel that looks for marine mammals or encounters them by chance; in the pack of every passenger on a whale-watching boat or cruise ship; in the glove box of every car that rolls onto a ferry or drives along the coast; in every school library; and under the Christmas tree of every nature lover.

Bernardo Alps
President, Los Angeles Chapter, American Cetacean Society

Introduction

In a recent television poll of the 10 things you "must do" before you die, the winner by a country mile was to swim with dolphins. This amazing finding clearly demonstrates our enduring fascination and affection for marine mammals. Since time immemorial, whales and dolphins have captured the imagination of poets, writers and mariners—so much so that you can find them woven into the folklore and legend of mankind the world over. As the renowned whaler and Arctic explorer Captain Scoresby wrote in 1820, "No branch of zoology is so much involved as that which is entitled cetology." Yet today whales and dolphins—cetaceans—still remain relatively little-known nomads of an oceanic realm and have evolved an aura and mystery of their own. They range in size from the diminutive Harbor Porpoise to the gargantuan Blue Whale, and include the strikingly beautiful Killer Whale.

Following centuries where marine mammals—cetaceans, seals and sea lions (pinnipeds)—were treated merely as a commodity to be exploited, public attitude has changed dramatically and these creatures are now recognized as important cohabitants of our increasingly fragile world. Over the last decade the interest in marine mammals has grown exponentially and this year an estimated 10 million people from 90 countries will take to the oceans to experience the thrill of watching whales, dolphins, seals and sea lions in the wild—and there is no better place to look for these magnificent creatures than along the western shores of North America.

The ocean waters of the Pacific adjacent to the coast of North America provide some of the finest and most accessible marine mammal watching in the world. At any time of the year it is possible to see a wide variety of marine mammals, including most of the planet's great whales, sometimes without even leaving the comfort of your car. You can sail within touching distance alongside friendly Gray Whales in Mexican lagoons or watch them from land as they migrate north along the coast to their summer feeding grounds off Alaska. You can encounter gigantic Blue Whales as they gorge on vast swarms of krill

in coastal waters of California, cruise with a super-pod of several thousand Risso's Dolphins over the Monterey Canyon or kayak among Killer Whales off the coast of British Columbia.

The ability to identify individual species is often the first step to appreciating the lives of marine mammals. But species identification is also the key to improving our knowledge about these animals, including their distribution, natural history and conservation requirements. This guide attempts to provide the very latest information on the identification of marine mammals at sea by illustrating them as they appear at the surface of the ocean. The aim of *Whales and Dolphins of the North American Pacific* is to enable anyone—expert or beginner—to identify marine mammals in the region. The text is definitive yet simple, and the photographs, many of which have never been published before, depict all the typical views of marine mammals in the wild. In addition, the section on behavior (page 31) is the most extensive ever produced in a field guide of this kind. It is designed both as an additional tool for identification and to help the observer discover why a particular surface maneuver may be taking place. Finally, the book gives a resumé of the principal marine mammal watching locations in the North American Pacific and includes a series of brief essays of very special marine mammal watching days at a selection of destinations in the region. We hope that these accounts will inspire you to make your own plans to explore the North American Pacific and meet whales, dolphins and other marine mammals up close. It is an exciting and powerful experience that can change forever your outlook on nature, and indeed life itself.

Although this book is designed to be used primarily as an identification guide to the marine mammals of the North American Pacific, it is also our hope that the splendid collection of photographs and illustrations represents a tribute to the animals themselves. We hope that you will be inspired by the magnificence and beauty of these creatures and help to ensure that they are conserved for generations to come.

Acknowledgements

Many people have assisted in the production of this book and our sincere thanks are due to them all. We intend to name everyone, but if we have inadvertently missed anyone we can only apologize. Despite the contribution of others, we hold full responsibility for any errors that may have crept in, and for any omissions that may have been made.

We would particularly like to thank Phil Coles for producing an excellent series of illustrations and Trevor Codlin and John Young for their advice on the photographic chapter. A special thanks must also go to contributing authors Heidi Pearson and Rick Harbo for sharing their "red letter days" with us and to Brian Clews for his detailed proofreading.

Many researchers gave generously of their time and answered many queries for us, and we would especially like to thank Charles Anderson, Robin W. Baird, Sascha Hooker, Jeremy Kiszka, C.D. MacLeod, Kelly Macleod, Merel Dalebout and Ursula Tscherter.

The production of this book would not have been possible without the help and cooperation of the photographers whose work is featured here. The outstanding images supplied are an intrinsic part of the guide and we would like to acknowledge the skill and patience of the following photographers who kindly allowed us to use their work: Simon Allen, Charles Anderson, Regina Asmutis-Silvia, Robin W. Baird, Frank S. Balthis, Cynde Bierman, Jean-Michel Bompar, Olivier Breysse, Alex Carlisle, Phillip Colla, Ron Evenden, Mark Fisher, David Fleetham, Don Getty, Alison Gill, Paula M. Gonzalez, Sierra Goodman, Steven Hajic, Bruce Hallett, Jennifer Harbo, Rick Harbo, Roger D. Harris, Hugh Harrop, Alan Henry, Donna Hertel, Matt Hobbs, Sascha Hooker, Thomas Jefferson, Morten Joergensen, C.D. MacLeod, Lori Mazzuca, George McCallum, Simon Mustoe, Dirk Neumann, Michael S. Nolan, Stephanie A. Norman, Phil Palmer, Gianni Pavan, Christopher Pearson, Heidi C. Pearson, Doug Perrine, Robert L. Pitman, Sue Rocca, Chris Shields, Jeff Skelton, Peggy Stap, Sam Taylor, Ralph Todd, Ursula Tscherter, Tom Walmsley, Pádraig Whooley, Kristi M. Willis, Alex Wilson and Gustavo Ybarra. Photographic credits start on page 208 of this guide. In addition to those photographers who are credited, we would like to thank all those who took the time and trouble to submit their photos for possible inclusion. We received many photographs of a very high standard and the final choice of images made has come down to the requirements of each chapter. It is fair to say that there were many more we would like to have used. Lastly, thanks to David and Terry at Max Communications for their help with scanning the images.

Finally, we are immensely grateful to Rob Still and Andy Swash of the **WILD**Guides team. We thank them for their enthusiasm and support throughout the preparation of this guide and their original ideas, which contributed immensely to the overall success of this project.

—*Graeme Cresswell, Dylan Walker and Todd Pusser*

Geography of the North American Pacific

The Pacific Ocean is the largest body of water on the planet, encompassing some 62.5 million square miles (100 million km^2) or roughly one-third of the Earth's surface. For the purposes of this guide the region known as the North American Pacific extends from southeastern Alaska south to the tip of Baja California, including the Gulf of California. This area of the Pacific is one of the most diverse regions of any stretch of ocean from a geographic and oceanographic point of view. This vast expanse of ocean is dominated by hundreds of islands, seamounts, submarine canyons and long stretches of mountainous coastline.

The coastline of southeastern Alaska and British Columbia is highly irregular and is dotted with hundreds of small mountainous islands. Volcanoes can be observed at numerous points along this stretch of coast. The sea floor that extends out from this coastline to a depth of 656 feet (200 m) is known as the continental shelf. The width of the continental shelf varies considerably in this region from less than 8 miles (13 km) to greater than 40 miles (65 km). At the edge of the shelf, the sea floor drops off suddenly into a steeper region known as the continental slope. Beyond the continental slope are the deepest waters of the North American Pacific. Known as the abyssal plain, the sea floor here is up to several miles deep.

Moving south along the coast of the US, the coastline from northwest Washington to central California is fairly regular with no islands to be found, apart from the Farallon Islands and tiny Año Neuvo near San Francisco. The width of the continental shelf varies from an average of 5 miles (8 km) south of Monterey, California, to greater than 50 miles (80 km) off Oregon. One of the most dominant features in the shelf along this stretch of coast is the Monterey Submarine Canyon in Monterey Bay, California. Submarine canyons are deep, V-shaped channels that cut the continental slope. The Monterey Submarine Canyon is the largest along the west coast of the US. It is roughly the size of the Grand Canyon in Arizona. The depth of this canyon ranges from just over 32 feet (10 m) at the mouth of the canyon just a ½ mile (1 km) off Moss Landing to over 9,843 feet (3,000 m) beyond the continental slope.

Other prominent geographical features of this region include a number of seamounts that can be found just off the coastline. Seamounts are submarine mountains that rise from the sea floor. These underwater mountains create an oasis of life along the abyssal plain and the continental slope by deflecting nutrient-carrying ocean currents upward, causing upwellings. These seamounts dot the offshore waters of the continental slope from Alaska to Baja California.

From Point Conception south along the coast of California the continental shelf is narrow. Prominent features in this region include the Channel Islands, Coronado Islands, Guadalupe Island and Cedros Island off Baja California.

The Sea of Cortez is a unique feature of this region and is one of the youngest and richest seas on Earth. It was formed some six million years ago when the Baja Peninsula tore away from the Mexican mainland through a process known as plate tectonics. The Baja Peninsula is located on the Pacific Plate while most of the mainland of Mexico and the US is attached to the North American Plate. As the Pacific Plate moved westward, the peninsula moved with it and continues to do so to this day. The rift that was formed between the Baja Peninsula and Mexico filled with water from the Pacific and formed the Sea of Cortez. This long, narrow body of water contains numerous islands and some of the strongest tides on the planet. The tidal flow produces upwelling, which contributes to the richness of the area. This is particularly evident around the Midriff Islands in the central Sea of Cortez. Here tidal currents speed up like rapids in between the islands creating turbulent flows that bring nutrient-rich water to the surface.

Aside from the geography of the North American Pacific, the single most dominant feature in the region is the California Current, which flows north to south from the Gulf of Alaska to Baja California. The current continues down the coast of Central America until it meets the Peru Current near the equator and begins to flow west away from the coastline. The intensity of the flow of the California Current varies throughout the year. During spring and summer, northwest winds blow against the current driving surface waters away from the coastline, bringing cooler, nutrient-rich waters up from the ocean depths. This upwelling plays a major role in the life cycles of many organisms and is crucial for the productivity of this region. During the fall and winter the prevailing winds begin to abate and the upwelling shuts down.

Every few years a phenomenon known as El Niño occurs. El Niño is associated with the Peru Current south of the equator in the eastern Pacific Ocean. During normal years, the Peru Current flows northward along the coast of South America and then westward across the Pacific Ocean toward Australia. But during El Niño years, the system fails. Trade winds along the equator that normally push the surface waters westward slow or even stop, causing a rise in sea surface temperature. This warm water begins to move north and spread throughout the eastern North Pacific. The upwellings that are common during normal years begin to diminish, thus decreasing the productivity in the region. El Niño is such a dominant feature that it affects weather patterns around the world.

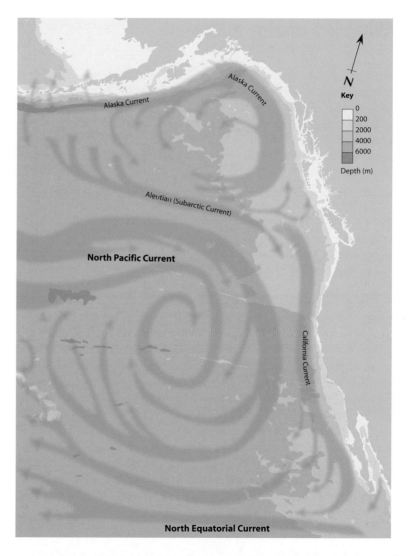

The currents of the eastern North Pacific Ocean in summer

What is a marine mammal?

A marine mammal is any mammal that makes its home in the sea for all or a substantial part of its life. Marine mammals, like all other members of the class Mammalia, are warm-blooded, breathe air through lungs and give birth to live young that are suckled by the mammary glands of the mother. All marine mammals are believed to have evolved from ancestors that lived on land. Such animals probably moved into the sea to take advantage of new food resources and were perhaps also seeking escape from terrestrial predators.

The term "marine mammal" is purely descriptive and is not a separate taxonomic designation. It encompasses mammals from three orders: Cetacea, Sirenia and Carnivora. The order Cetacea consists entirely of whales, dolphins and porpoises; the order Sirenia comprises the sea cows: and the order Carnivora includes polar bears, seals, sea lions and sea otters. In total, there are approximately 120 species of marine mammals throughout the world, of which over a third are found in the North American Pacific.

Marine mammals can reach a far greater size than land mammals, with the largest whales reaching a staggering length of 105 feet (32 m) and weighing in excess of 154 tons (140 metric tonnes). This is a distinct advantage in water where a lower surface area to volume ratio minimizes heat loss from the body surface.

Of all the marine mammals the cetaceans are best adapted for life in water. Pinnipeds (seals and sea lions), sea otters and polar bears are dependent upon land or ice to breed. Since cetaceans live permanently in water, their size is not limited by the effects of gravity, unlike terrestrial mammals. Rather than supporting body weight, the limbs of cetaceans have been modified into flippers and tail flukes and are used primarily for propulsion and control of movement through the water. Other adaptations to the underwater environment include the development of a thick blubber layer for insulation and the migration of nostrils to the top of the head to form one or two blowholes. In addition, cetaceans have a highly developed sense of hearing,

and communicate with each other by producing a variety of sounds. The toothed cetaceans are also able to locate their prey using echolocation—a system similar to the one used by bats to find their way around in the dark. By emitting short pulses of sound that bounce off nearby objects, toothed cetaceans are able to build up a picture of their surroundings. The pulses of sound are produced in the nasal sac just inside the blowhole.

Although they spend considerable periods of their lives in water, pinnipeds have to return to land or ice in order to give birth and this has restricted their degree of aquatic specialization. Like cetaceans, they have developed a streamlined shape and their limbs have been modified to form flippers. However, pinnipeds have extensive hair over the body surface and their limbs are used for propulsion in water and on land. Both cetaceans and pinnipeds have reduced or eliminated protruding body parts that create drag, such as large external ears or reproductive organs and mammary glands. Like other carnivorous mammals, pinnipeds are intelligent, with well-developed senses. Seals have large eyes in relation to body size and good underwater vision, adaptable to the darkness of ocean depths. Their hearing is also excellent in both air and water.

Sirenians no longer occur in the North American Pacific and the polar bear is primarily restricted to the Arctic. Besides the cetaceans and the pinnipeds, the only other marine mammal to occur in the North American Pacific is the Sea Otter. This species belongs to the order Carnivora and, like pinnipeds, is an excellent swimmer, foraging exclusively in water. Like other members of the family Mustelidae, the Sea Otter has a relatively long, thin body with short legs, but it is the only member of its family to spend its whole life in the marine environment. Sea Otters are distinct from all pinnipeds in the structure of their hind limbs and fore limbs—Sea Otters have separate toes on their limbs while pinnipeds have digits that are joined by skin webbing or cartilage.

Identification features of marine mammals

BALEEN WHALE
Humpback Whale (above) and
Common Minke Whale (below)

Baleen plates

Throat grooves
(rorquals only)

Double blowhole

Rostrum

Upper lip

Lower lip

Jawline

TOOTHED CETACEAN
Short-beaked Common Dolphin

Single blowhole

Melon

Forehead

Beak

Dorsal fin

Back

Tail stock

Tail flukes

Notch

Pectoral fin
(flipper)

Flank

Belly

PINNIPED
California Sea Lion (female, left) and
Northern Fur Seal (male, right)

Ear flaps

Muzzle

Whiskers

Sagittal crest

Mane

Back

Fore flipper

Hind flipper

Getting started—finding marine mammals

It is very easy to become hooked on watching marine mammals—and once you are, you will never look at the sea in the same way again! For dedicated marine mammal watchers, there is always more to the ocean than a fiery sunset or a curling wave. Whether you are walking along a beach or standing on a headland or a boat, you will find yourself scanning for a raised fin, arching body or distant blow. Finding marine mammals usually requires a dose of knowledge, an optimistic outlook and a sprinkle of good luck. This chapter will help to get you started by providing information on when, where and how to look.

When

Although marine mammals spend much of their time underwater, they must return to the surface to breathe on a regular basis. The amount of time spent at the surface varies greatly from species to species and also depends on whether the animal is resting, feeding or traveling. In some species there is no clear diurnal pattern of behavior, but in others their activities are influenced by the time of day. For example, some deep-diving cetaceans spend more time at the surface during daylight hours when prey species retreat to the safety of deeper waters. By waiting until nightfall to feed, they expend less energy on diving as their prey migrate closer to the surface.

Marine mammals are generally easier to find in some seasons than in others. Different species occur in different waters in different months, so the dedicated marine mammal watcher is likely to encounter a greater diversity of species by watching in all seasons. It is widely accepted that in temperate regions of the world, including much of the North American Pacific, summer is the best time to watch. There are several reasons for this: high-pressure weather systems often settle for considerable periods, bringing warm, sunny and windless conditions; the sea is generally at its calmest; and day length is at its greatest, allowing more time for watching.

As the summer progresses these factors combine to increase water temperature, allowing phytoplankton (the "green grass" of the marine ecosystem) to flourish. Warm, sunny conditions enable these free-floating marine plants to increase in numbers dramatically, providing food, either directly or indirectly, for all other marine creatures whether microscopic zooplankton or 100-ton whales. At lower latitudes, in the subtropical waters of the North American Pacific, the effect of the seasons is reversed, with a number of species arriving from temperate waters for the winter months. It is at this time of year that the majority of whale-watching takes place.

There are also other factors that influence the distribution of marine mammals. One of the most significant is the need to find a safe place to give birth and raise young. Marine mammals, particularly some large whales and some pinnipeds, are capable of traveling great distances to arrive at specific mating and calving grounds. As a result, the seal rookeries scattered along the entire length

Because Short-finned Pilot Whales feed predominantly at night, they are able to spend much of the day resting and socializing at the surface.

of the North American Pacific and the Gray Whale calving lagoons on the coast of Baja California provide predictable marine mammal watching opportunities at specific times of the year.

Where

With the exception of pinniped rookeries and Sea Otter territories, which are often present in the same location for many years, marine mammals tend to be sparsely distributed and difficult to find. Like their mammalian relatives on land, they are at or near the top of the food chain, occurring at low densities over large areas. Knowing where to look is therefore very important.

Some marine mammals favour shallow waters or coastal areas, whereas others restrict themselves to very deep water. Some are resident, while others are migratory. With experience and the aid of a marine chart and a global positioning system (GPS), which enables an exact location to be pinpointed on the chart, it is possible to determine the habitat preferences of each species of marine mammal. This in turn may assist with identification. For example, the Dwarf Sperm Whale and the Harbor Porpoise are both small and gray, with a prominent dorsal fin, and move lethargically at the surface. However, they live in very different habitats; Harbor Porpoises are generally restricted to shelf waters, often close to shore, whereas Dwarf Sperm Whales are much more likely to be encountered in deep offshore waters.

While water depth and oceanographic features can be useful indicators of the habitat of a particular species, location alone should not be used as a way of identifying a marine mammal specifically. Part of the joy of watching marine mammals is their complete unpredictability. It is almost impossible to guess where they will occur because they can pop up anywhere at any time. Marine mammals do not follow any rules. They roam freely over great distances and there is still much to learn about their distribution and migratory patterns. For the marine mammal watcher, the most important principle is to put in as much effort as possible. The longer you watch, the better your chances of seeing something. It's as simple as that!

By using a global positioning system (GPS) and a marine chart, it is possible to learn about the habitat preferences of marine mammals.

Whale-watchers sight a group of dolphins.

TYPICAL DISTRIBUTION OF MARINE MAMMAL SPECIES IN THE NORTH AMERICAN PACIFIC

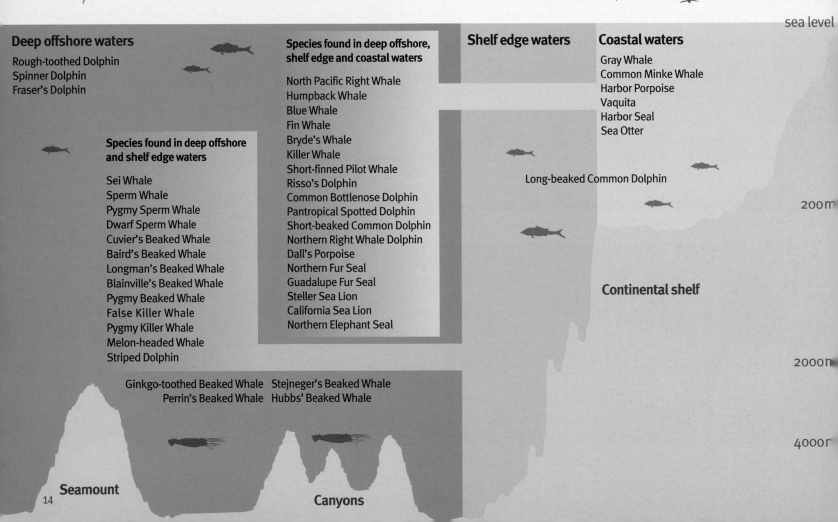

sea level

Deep offshore waters

Rough-toothed Dolphin
Spinner Dolphin
Fraser's Dolphin

Species found in deep offshore and shelf edge waters

Sei Whale
Sperm Whale
Pygmy Sperm Whale
Dwarf Sperm Whale
Cuvier's Beaked Whale
Baird's Beaked Whale
Longman's Beaked Whale
Blainville's Beaked Whale
Pygmy Beaked Whale
False Killer Whale
Pygmy Killer Whale
Melon-headed Whale
Striped Dolphin

Species found in deep offshore, shelf edge and coastal waters

North Pacific Right Whale
Humpback Whale
Blue Whale
Fin Whale
Bryde's Whale
Killer Whale
Short-finned Pilot Whale
Risso's Dolphin
Common Bottlenose Dolphin
Pantropical Spotted Dolphin
Short-beaked Common Dolphin
Northern Right Whale Dolphin
Dall's Porpoise
Northern Fur Seal
Guadalupe Fur Seal
Steller Sea Lion
California Sea Lion
Northern Elephant Seal

Shelf edge waters

Coastal waters

Gray Whale
Common Minke Whale
Harbor Porpoise
Vaquita
Harbor Seal
Sea Otter

Long-beaked Common Dolphin

Continental shelf

200m

2000m

4000m

Ginkgo-toothed Beaked Whale   Stejneger's Beaked Whale
Perrin's Beaked Whale   Hubbs' Beaked Whale

Seamount

Canyons

14

How

Marine mammal watchers in the North American Pacific are spoiled for choice in terms of the number of sites to visit, species to see and commercial operators running trips.

Whether you simply wish to see a whale, a dolphin or a seal, or target a particular species, a little preparation prior to your trip can make a lot of difference. Below is a priority list of things to do in order to get the very most out of your whale-watching trip, although many of the key points can also be applied to watching pinniped rookeries and haulout sites.

1 Do some background reading to find out the best season and location to see your target species, or to combine marine mammal watching with your other leisure time activities.

2 Once you have decided on a location, try to find out which operators are running whale-watching trips in the area. This information is easily accessible through literature, websites, and tourist information centers.

3 Choose an operator. The type of whale-watching experience will be influenced greatly by the operator that you choose. Again, research your operator through available literature, websites and tourist information centers, as well as phoning the operator for further information, contacting friends who have previously visited the area, or asking for recommendations from local residents and tourists on arrival. Alternatively, try several operators to discover which one suits you best.

4 Whale-watching is unpredictable in many ways so putting time into planning your trip often pays off. Check with the operator to see whether you need to reserve tickets in advance. Some trips are very popular, particularly on weekends or during holidays, but if ticket reservation is not required, this gives you the flexibility to check on the weather before making a final

Watching a Bryde's Whale

Questions to ask whale-watch operators

1 How much does the trip cost?

2 How long does the trip last?

3 What type and size of vessel do you use?

4 Is the trip designed for whale-watching, or is whale-watching just part of the tour?

5 When and from where do you depart?

6 Is there a professional naturalist guide onboard? This is an important influence on the quality of your experience. A good guide will provide information on the marine mammals of the area and how to identify them.

7 Is the boat used for marine mammal research and do you contribute to the conservation of the animals that you watch?

8 How often do you see marine mammals? Which species and when?

9 How many people do you carry per trip and are you confident that there will be enough reservations for the trip to run?

10 Do you provide a free return ticket if no marine mammals are seen?

decision. Don't be afraid to phone up operators and ask them what they have been seeing over the last few days. Several operators based in the same port may have different itineraries and, consequently, could be encountering different marine mammals.

⑤ It is often possible to increase your chances of seeing a particular species by explaining to an operator what you are attempting to do, particularly if you are prepared to make several trips to achieve your goal. Whale-watch operators like to satisfy their customers but are generally not used to people with specific requests. They will try to help you if they can.

⑥ Many people spend considerable resources on travel and accommodation in order to go whale-watching and then only take one trip. While this may satisfy the curiosity of some, it is unusual for a return trip to result in exactly the same type of encounters. Why not take two, three or even four trips out with the same operator on the same day, or over several days? Not only are you likely to see different animals, species and behaviors, but by building up a rapport with the crew you may gain a greater insight into marine mammals and the lives of those people who make a living from the sea. If you do decide to take several return trips, try to negotiate a discounted rate in return for your multiple booking.

When searching for marine mammals it is very important to choose a good place from which to watch. On land, the best locations are headlands with a reasonably high vantage point, particularly those which extend to deep water. A good tip is to seek out lighthouses, which are often built on the most prominent headlands. Binoculars and often a telescope are useful tools for land-based watching. Most coastal areas are visited by marine mammals annually but some regions entertain a greater diversity and abundance of species than others. The best locations are blessed with the year-round presence of Common Bottlenose Dolphins, Killer Whales, Harbor Seals or Sea Otters. Other sites are visited occasionally or seasonally, such as during the Gray Whale migration. Land-based watching generally requires patience and concentration while scanning the sea systematically. With experience you will discover the best weather, time of day and season to watch. If you are prepared to put in the time, land-based watching can be extremely rewarding, especially as you can watch marine mammals without disturbing them. It's also absolutely free!

If you are watching from a boat you should always carry binoculars. The bridge and close to the bow are good places from which to search, since this allows for observation ahead of the vessel. A stable platform is necessary in order to use binoculars without too much shake. Elevation is also an important consideration, particularly in rougher seas when a high vantage point allows the observer to track cetaceans as they travel through wave troughs. Also consider gaining shelter from the wind, reducing glare from the sun and avoiding sea spray.

Finding marine mammals requires a great deal of patience. Keep searching over the same area of water even if you think there is nothing there. Some

Often positioned on prominent headlands, lighthouses, such as this one at Point Reyes, California, can be excellent for land-based marine mammal watching.

Wispy cirrus clouds over an Alaskan skyline indicate a fine day for whale-watching.

cetaceans and pinnipeds can stay underwater for an hour or more before eventually surfacing, and even when animals remain at the surface it is surprising how easy it can be to miss them. For example, a 49-foot-long (15-m) Sperm Whale is easily overlooked when afloat with only a small proportion of its upper back showing.

Watching marine mammals is generally easiest in relatively calm weather. A sea state of three or less, when there are few or no whitecaps to the waves is preferable. In these conditions, large whales and leaping dolphins are often first noticed because of the white water they create on surfacing. The blow is another feature that can help locate a large whale. Blows can be seen several miles away and may hang in the air for several seconds. Having observed an unusual splash, a possible blow or a dark shape in the water, check with your binoculars. It may be nothing but more often than not your first impressions will have been correct and you will have found a marine mammal!

Weather

The sun's glare, fog, sea swell, rain and wind can all affect the chances of locating marine mammals at sea, but by far the most important factor is the sea state. Sea state is the term used to describe the wave formation created by the wind. A sea state of three or less, when the waves have few or no whitecaps, is generally considered to be most conducive to marine mammal watching. Anything higher and it is certainly easy to miss small and unobtrusive species such as the diminutive Harbor Porpoise.

Sea state can be measured using the guide on the next page:

A guide to sea states

0 *Mirror calm; whale-watching heaven!*

1 *Slight ripples; no white water*

2 *Small wavelets; glassy crests, no whitecaps*

3 *Large wavelets; crests begin to break, few whitecaps*

4 *Longer waves; many whitecaps; whale-watching becomes more tricky*

5 *Moderate waves of longer form; some spray*

6 *Large waves; many whitecaps; frequent spray; whale-watching very difficult*

7 *Sea heaps up; white foam blows in streaks*

8 *Long, high waves; edges breaking; foam blows in streaks*

9 *High waves; sea begins to roll; dense foam streaks; scary!*

Equipment

Being cold, wet, seasick and miserable can take the edge off a spectacular marine mammal encounter. Fortunately, such situations can largely be avoided by wearing the correct clothing and packing the right equipment for the trip.

The most important considerations are the bare essentials: warm dry clothes, food and water. Even if it is a hot calm day on land, weather conditions at sea can be deceptively cool and changeable. As a general rule try to dress for all weather. Take several layers of clothing, which will improve insulation in cold weather and give you several options if it is warm. Always think ahead. Once you have a chill it can be difficult to warm up, even with extra layers of clothing, so put warm clothes on as soon as you start to feel cold. A hat will prevent around 35% of your body heat being lost through your head. Windproof or waterproof clothing is essential. Some operators will also insist on soft-soled shoes, which will give you a better grip on deck. In sunny weather, a cap, sunglasses and sunscreen are advisable for protection. To avoid seasickness it is important to remain hydrated with a full stomach, so take plenty of non-alcoholic drink and snack food with you. If you feel seasick, it can help to eat, even if you don't feel like it.

Much of a whale-watching trip may be spent traveling to and from marine mammal hot spots. You may wish to read a book, look for seabirds and other marine life or simply watch the sea in its ever-changing form. Whale-watch operators will often ask for your help in searching for marine mammals. With perseverance you may well be the first to spot something!

Binoculars are the most important piece of equipment for watching marine mammals.

Apart from a good field guide, binoculars are the most essential piece of equipment for observing marine mammals. They can be used to scan the sea at distance, and they increase your chances of observing subtle behaviors or identification features that would go undetected with the naked eye. If possible, buy a good pair of binoculars that feel comfortable and are not too heavy, with a magnification of between 7x and 10x and a wide field of view. The field of view is especially important as locating objects at sea can be difficult due to the uniformity of the background. Spotting telescopes are very useful for land-based watching and can also be used on large stable vessels. However, they are best used in conjunction with binoculars, which are generally more suitable for scanning the sea because they have a much wider field of view. For information on video and camera equipment see page 20.

The checklist to the right details the main requirements for a boat-based marine mammal watching trip.

Spotting scopes are very useful for land-based watching.

Equipment checklist

Warm clothes
Waterproof / windproof outer garments
Hat / cap
Sunglasses (polarized glasses help viewing through water)
Rubber-soled shoes for grip
Waterproof backpack
Binoculars
Still camera equipment (two camera bodies, lenses, spare battery, ample film or memory cards, polarizing filter)
Video camera equipment
Lens cloth
Food
Water
Seasickness tablets, pressure bands or medication
Notebook and pen / pencil

Taking photographs and video footage

Capturing images of marine mammals

Taking good photographs of marine mammals requires technical understanding, field craft and patience, but the results can be immensely exciting. Not only does capturing a marine mammal on film provide a permanent record of an encounter, but with today's digital cameras it is increasingly easy to produce photographs of publishable standard. And with so many marine mammal discoveries still to be made, you could even be lucky enough to capture something completely unique!

As well as being an artistic medium, photography is an important scientific tool in its own right. By taking photographs of individually recognizable features such as the shape of a whale's tail flukes or the markings on its dorsal fin, scientists have been able to study the activities of cetaceans in the wild without unduly affecting their behavior. Increasingly, members of the public are being asked to contribute to these "photo-identification catalogs" to help us all learn more about the lives of these mysterious creatures.

Selecting photographic equipment

Selecting the appropriate camera gear and film is the essential first step to taking good photographs. Although adequate photographs can be taken during close encounters by using a compact camera with a zoom lens, marine mammals often remain too distant for these cameras to be of use. A single lens reflex (SLR) camera is ideal, being compact and durable with a range of attachable lenses, allowing you to take telephoto, zoom or wide angle images on the same body.

Most SLRs also have a motor drive which enables the camera to take a rapid sequence of images capable of capturing fast-moving activity such as breaching. For these reasons the SLR gives you the flexibility required for photographing marine mammals.

The proximity of the subject is often unpredictable, so a choice of lenses is useful. If a marine mammal is close, a standard or wide-angle lens may be appropriate. Given that encounters are often brief, having two camera bodies with different lenses will help save time at the crucial moment. Of the fixed telephoto lenses, a 200-mm lens is often the most useful. However, some photographers prefer to use a zoom lens, such as the 75–300-mm, as this provides the flexibility to take photographs at close and medium ranges. Lenses with a higher magnification generally require a tripod for stability, so they are inappropriate for boat-based photography.

Another important factor in choosing your lens is its light-gathering capacity. Remember that slow shutter speeds increase the chances of a blurred image due to movement of the boat or the animal as the photograph is taken. The speed of the shutter is also affected by the type of film used. Higher-speed film requires less light but generally results in a grainier photograph. To achieve shutter speeds of 1/250 to 1/500 of a second or faster in good to moderate light conditions with a 70–300mm lens, a film of ASA/ISO 100 or 200 should be sufficient.

Land-based photography

A surprising number of marine mammals, including all pinnipeds, Sea Otters and several species of cetaceans, can be photographed from land in certain locations and seasons. The skills and equipment required to photograph them are quite different from those needed at sea. Using cameras with long telephoto lenses mounted on tripods helps to avoid disturbing animals as photographs can be taken over a greater distance. The movements and behavior of the animals may change with the time of day and the state of the tide, so taking the time to study them will help you to compose better images.

Boat-based photography

For the majority of photographers, boats provide the most accessible platform for getting close to marine mammals, though they also present a number of unique challenges for the photographer. Taking good photographs of marine mammals at sea requires a large degree of patience, experience and above all, luck!

Camera and video equipment will help you make the most of your encounters.

Producing that dream photograph is as much about being in the right place at the right time as it is about the type of photographic equipment and film used. There is no substitute for experience, so there is no need to be afraid to experiment with shutter speeds, exposures and filters when photographing.

The first priority on boarding the boat is to find the best place from which to take photographs. As a general rule, try to be near to the bow but avoid areas that are less stable or where sea spray could be a problem. If you are unsure, ask a member of the crew to recommend a good spot. Above all, position yourself where you have the most freedom to move. You don't want to be trapped on the port side while a whale is breaching off the starboard side. On a rocking boat, find a place where your body is safely supported, leaving your hands free to operate the camera safely without risk of personal injury or damage to your equipment. It is also worth considering your position in relation to the sea surface. Most photographs are taken from as close to the water as possible, as this shows the animal as another surfacing marine mammal might see it. However, photographs taken from an elevated position have the advantage of revealing the shape and color of submerged parts of the animal.

Before any animals are located, practice metering against the sea and other objects. Get an idea of the shutter speeds and aperture you are likely to need in the light conditions you are experiencing. If possible, aim for shutter speeds of 1/500 of a second or faster. This will allow you to photograph fast-moving dolphins or whales from a rocking boat. Slow moving whales such as Humpbacks can be photographed at shutter speeds as slow as 1/250 of a second.

Predicting where a marine mammal will surface is essential to taking good photographs. Different species move in different ways and so there is no substitute for experience. The crew of a whale-watching boat are often able to tell where a marine mammal is going to surface before you can, so stand where you can hear them talking. The captain may even have a favored side of the boat, which is placed alongside surfacing animals.

For the best color, try to take photographs with the sun behind you. Taking an early-morning or late-afternoon whale-watching trip will help. However, the middle of the day is the best time to photograph down through the water. This is particularly useful when dolphins are bow riding or a whale approaches the boat. Attaching filters to the lens can help to reduce glare and reflection and protect the lens from spray or even whale blows should you be lucky enough to get that close! It is also possible to protect your equipment by purchasing waterproof covers for cameras that still allow you to manage the controls.

Despite the fact that as a photographer, the position of the boat and the marine mammal are out of your control, it is still important to consider composition. Once you have the animal in range, attempt to get the horizon level in your viewfinder. If possible, give the image perspective. Photographs of marine mammals with boats, land or seabirds in the background increase the interest of the image and provide a sense of scale.

When photographing from a whale-watching vessel, always be courteous to the people around you. They have just as much right as you do to watch from the primary viewing areas and may not appreciate your lens obscuring their view. If the boat is crowded or the animals distant, try to take time out to enjoy and appreciate the experience. Ultimately, this will improve your ability as a marine mammal photographer. In the meantime, remember that every photographic opportunity is a learning experience and something to be enjoyed as an integral part of watching these fascinating animals.

How to identify marine mammals

Beginner to expert

Marine mammals include a diverse selection of species, ranging from strikingly unique to nearly identical in appearance. As a result they are an ideal group to tackle no matter what your experience. For example, it would be difficult to mistake a bull Killer Whale or a Sea Otter for anything else, and yet the craft of identifying pinnipeds at sea is still in its infancy and several species of beaked whale have yet to be reliably described alive. Marine mammals are unusual animals to attempt to identify because, when at sea, only a proportion of the animal tends to be in view at any one time. To add to the challenge, the differences between species are often subtle and views may be brief before the animal dives.

Marine mammal identification has progressed greatly over the last 20 years but there is still much to learn, with new sightings regularly contributing to and furthering our current understanding. With the increase in popularity of whale-watching, the craft of marine mammal identification has advanced significantly. Learning how to identify marine mammals is good fun, and is bound to further your enjoyment of these magnificent creatures. To begin, all you have to do is read this chapter, which highlights the key features and behaviors to look out for—then start watching!

Look for a combination of features

When watching marine mammals try to avoid basing your identification on one assumption. Picking out a number of clues will increase your chances of reaching a correct identification. Using a combination of features is also important because marine mammals are unpredictable, sometimes contradicting one or more "typical" identification features. Deep-water species will turn up in the shallows; non-fluking whales will raise their tail flukes prior to a dive; freakish colors and patterns occasionally occur; and even hybridization has been recorded with individuals showing some features attributable to two different species. When identifying marine mammals it is important to be aware of all the possibilities and take nothing for granted.

Rewriting the rule book

Basing identification on one assumption could lead to pitfalls like the following:

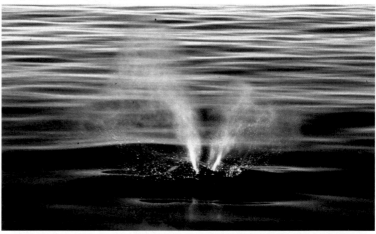

The wrong whale: *This Humpback Whale emitted an unusual V-shaped blow, normally assigned to the North Pacific Right Whale.*

The white whale: *Although Humpback Whales are described as black or dark gray in color, white individuals have been recorded.*

Fins revealed: *This Baird's Beaked Whale appears to have a large dorsal fin. In fact, the animal is revealing one half of its tail flukes while swimming on its side.*

Look upon each encounter as building on your previous experience. As with all wildlife watching, there is no substitute for spending time in the field. It is easy to be frustrated by a brief view of a marine mammal after a long wait, and to be tempted to put a name to it when you are unable to see all of the features required to do so. Such temptations can only be detrimental in learning your craft. Instead, take a precautionary approach, and be thankful that you have encountered a marine mammal, even if you are unsure of the species. A good observer looks for as many features as possible, records the details of their sighting accurately and is not afraid to categorize a marine mammal as "unidentified," "possible" or "probable" if they are not entirely confident of the species' identity. You might not realize it, but every sighting is a learning opportunity which will improve your chances of a positive identification at the next attempt.

Taking notes

Learning to take detailed and accurate notes in a logbook or diary will help you to really analyze marine mammals and fix their characteristics in your mind. However tempting it is to rush to your field guide after an encounter with an unidentified marine mammal, try to resist doing so until you have noted down all of the features that you saw, preferably also making a sketch. Flicking through your field guide before making notes can cloud your judgement. Take

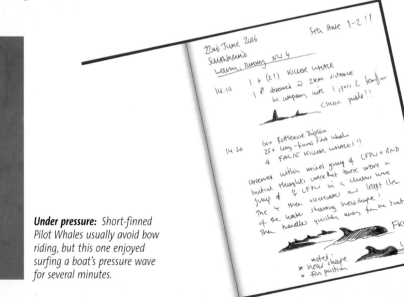

Under pressure: *Short-finned Pilot Whales usually avoid bow riding, but this one enjoyed surfing a boat's pressure wave for several minutes.*

notes immediately after the encounter, and record as many features as possible. These should include the date, time, sea and weather conditions, distance to the sighting, location (exact latitude and longitude if possible), and reference numbers for any photographs taken. Afterward, consider transferring your notes to a diary with detailed records of your sightings. This will provide you with a reminder of great encounters and a useful reference resource for the future.

If you have a camera, photographing or filming an encounter allows you to attempt the identification at your leisure, consulting field guides and past notes. If the species is rare, photographs and video footage are the best way to prove beyond doubt that you have correctly identified it.

Key features to look for

Sightings of marine mammals are often brief. Concentrate on key features to help with identification. In approximate order of importance, these are:

Size

Due to the relatively uniform nature of the sea, judging the size of a surfacing marine mammal can be difficult. Try to compare the size of the animal with other familiar objects at a similar distance, such as fishing boats or seabirds. Remember that only a small portion of the back is generally visible above the surface at any one time. Size should also be interpreted with caution because it may vary with the age and sex of the individual.

Comparing a marine mammal with an object of known size such as a boat or seabird can help in estimating its size. The size of these Humpback Whales can be compared to a whale-watching boat and a dolphin (left) and the wingspan of Sooty Shearwaters (right).

Shape

Marine mammals come in many shapes, ranging from long and slim, through rotund and bulky, to short and stocky. It is therefore very important to try to judge the shape of an animal. In addition to the overall body shape, the shape of appendages is often diagnostic. For example, sightings of pinniped species at sea often involve only the head raised above the water so the shape of the head and the presence or absence of ears are important features to look out for.

Humpback Whale: *Stocky animal with long pectoral flippers.*

Sea Otter: *A relatively long-bodied mammal with a broad head, large flipper-like hind limbs, short fore limbs and a long, flattened tail.*

Northern Elephant Seal: *Very robustly built with a very large head and proportionately short fore limbs (flippers).*

Long-beaked Common Dolphin: *Streamlined body with a long, slender beak and a tall, backward-curved dorsal fin.*

Dorsal fin

In cetaceans, the size, shape and position of the dorsal fin is a very useful aid to identification. Apart from the North Pacific Right Whale, Gray Whale and Northern Right Whale Dolphin, all cetaceans in the North American Pacific show a dorsal fin. The shape of this fin may vary greatly both within and between species and can be triangular, sickle-shaped or merely a hump. Try to determine the size of the fin in relation to the length of the body, its position along the back and, in large whales, its appearance at the surface in relation to the blowhole (see also Surfacing sequences on page 36).

Killer Whale: *Broad and triangular, reaching up to 2 m in height in adult males.*

Blow

In many of the large cetaceans, a tall jet of water is expelled as the animal surfaces and breathes out. This is known as the blow, the size and shape of which is variable depending upon the species and the individual's activity. For further details and a full comparison of cetacean blows turn to page 32.

Sperm Whale: *No fin, just a small hump.*

Dwarf Sperm Whale: *Broad at the base, generally with a blunt tip, although sometimes pointed.*

Fin Whale: *Broad-based, swept back and often blunt at the tip.*

Harbor Porpoise: *Small, low and triangular with a blunt tip.*

Pacific White-sided Dolphin: *Typically tall, strongly backward-curved and broad at the base.*

Risso's Dolphin: *Backward-curved and tall in relation to body length.*

Coloration and patterning

The color and patterning on a marine mammal can be difficult to judge, especially at sea where the angle of the sun and the weather can create different impressions. Often the observer may be reduced to using the terms light and dark as a description. Patterning is of great importance in the identification of some marine mammals, particularly members of the dolphin family, which can otherwise appear very similar.

The colors and patterns on the flanks of these dolphins provide the observer with reliable and diagnostic features.

Pacific White-sided Dolphin: *Body is black, gray and white with a thin black pencil-line separating the flanks from the belly. Another gray pencil-line runs along the upper back.*

Northern Bottlenose Whales: *The color appears very different in varying light conditions. The photographs are of the same two animals (shown together at the bottom of the plate) and were all taken on the same day.*

Risso's Dolphin: *The only dolphin with pale coloration and extensive criss-cross scarring all over the body.*

Short-beaked Common Dolphin: *The most striking identification feature is the characteristic "hourglass" pattern on the flanks.*

Long-beaked Common Dolphin: *Very similar to Short-beaked Common Dolphin but the color pattern is more muted with a less crisp demarcation between the dark back and the pale flanks.*

Pantropical Spotted Dolphin: *Most easily identified by its spotting, a unique feature among cetaceans of the North American Pacific.*

Striped Dolphin: *A distinctive pale blaze sweeps from the flank up toward the dorsal fin, and a thin, dark stripe runs along the lower flank.*

Number and composition

The number of animals and composition of a group, especially the number of young animals, can provide important clues to identification for some species. For example, the very similar Pygmy Killer Whale and Melon-headed Whale generally occur in different group sizes, with usually only Melon-headed Whale in pods of more than 50 animals. The presence of young in a group of Sperm Whales can also assist in their identification, as such an occurrence is only likely in warm temperate to tropical waters. Beware though, that mixed species groups can easily be misidentified as adults and young of the same species. Here, a group of Pacific White-sided Dolphins is dwarfed by several Risso's Dolphins traveling alongside them.

Behavior

Observing and understanding behavior is an important part of the identification process in cetaceans, pinnipeds and otters. Marine mammals exhibit a wide variety of interesting behaviors, which are covered in detail on pages 31–65.

Behavior

Due to the difficulties and expense of studying marine mammals at sea, our understanding of their behavior has largely concentrated on shore-based colonies in the case of pinnipeds and nearshore resident populations in the case of cetaceans and Sea Otters.

Current knowledge of marine mammals at sea is based almost entirely on observations made while the animals are at the surface. Fortunately for whale-watchers and scientists, all marine mammals must surface to breathe, affording the observer a glimpse into the lives of a group of animals that spend much of their time in the mysterious depths. Just how much of a glimpse depends on a number of factors, such as whether the marine mammal is feeding, resting or diving, and whether it is shy of vessels, indifferent or actively approaches them.

The duration of a marine mammal's dive is one of the most important factors affecting the chances of encountering it. The Harbor Porpoise is one of the smallest cetaceans and is capable of staying underwater for only a few minutes; this means that it appears at the surface regularly but only needs to surface a few times in order to catch its breath for another descent. At the other extreme, the Sperm Whale may dive as deep as 1.9 miles (3 km) and remain submerged for over an hour. This behavior will reduce the chances of the whale being observed. However, long dive times also require longer recovery times and the Sperm Whale may spend 10 minutes or more resting at the surface before it embarks on another deep dive.

Fortunately for us the surface of the sea has much more to offer marine mammals than the opportunity to catch their breath. Many species are highly social and exhibit a variety of interesting and distinct behaviors at the surface. While some of these behaviors are not fully understood, our knowledge of them has increased dramatically in recent years.

The behavior of marine mammals can also be used to aid identification. For

Killer Whale breaching.

example, some large whales such as the Blue, Humpback, Gray, North Pacific Right and Sperm Whales regularly raise their tail flukes on diving in a behavior known as fluking. However, fluking is only rarely observed in Fin, Sei, Bryde's and Common Minke Whales.

All of the regularly observed surface behaviors of marine mammals are described in detail in this section. Where possible, species demonstrating the same behavior are illustrated so that direct comparisons can be made between them for identification purposes. Understanding behavior will add an extra dimension to your observations and help you to get the most out of the encounters you may have.

Blowing or spouting: *The breath of a cetacean, in which moisture-laden air is expelled from the lungs as a visible spout of water.*

Blowing or spouting

The moisture-laden breath released from the top of the head of a cetacean is called the blow or spout. In toothed cetaceans the blow is expelled from a single nostril (blowhole), while in baleen whales the blow is emitted from a pair of nostrils (blowholes). The blow, which is a combination of vapor and seawater, is quickly followed by a sharp intake of air before the cetacean holds its breath and dives. When surfacing to breathe, most cetaceans rise several times in succession before diving for a period of between a few minutes and over an hour.

In many of the larger cetaceans, the blow is visible as a tall jet of water expelled vertically as the animal surfaces and breathes out. The size and shape of the blow and the sequence of blows varies between species and with the activity of the individual. Blows may be visible over several kilometers and may hang in the air for as

long as a minute. Early whalers were well aware that the blow is often the first sign of the presence of a large cetacean, as illustrated by the famous whaling phrase "thar she blows." Even at distance, blows can be an important first clue to identification. However, because they are highly variable and may be affected by the wind, waves, air temperature and light, they should generally not be used in isolation to identify a cetacean to species level.

Blue Whale *(above and left)*
Largest blow of all; an enormous vertical column up to 39 feet (12 m) tall.

Fin Whale
Very tall column-shaped blow; thicker and taller than Sei Whale, but smaller than Blue Whale.

Sei Whale
Tall, thin and vertical blow; less robust and usually lower than Fin Whale.

Bryde's Whale
Tall, thin and vertical blow; similar in size to Sei Whale.

Humpback Whale
Variable blow; tall, vertical and bushy.

Common Minke Whale
Small, vertical and bushy blow, but usually not visible.

Gray Whale
Tall and bushy blow; may appear V-shaped or heart-shaped.

North Pacific Right Whale
Distinctive, tall, V-shaped blow.

Sperm Whale
Moderately tall and bushy blow, angled forward.

Longman's Beaked Whale
Short and bushy blow, angled slightly forward.

Cuvier's Beaked Whale
Short and bushy blow, angled slightly forward.

Blainville's Beaked Whale
Short and bushy blow, angled slightly forward.

Killer Whale
Moderately tall and bushy blow.

Short-finned Pilot Whale
Short and bushy blow.

False Killer Whale
Short and bushy blow.

Melon-headed Whale
Inconspicuous, short and bushy blow.

Fluking

Some species of whale regularly raise their tail flukes vertically into the air as they dive. The shape and color of the flukes and the patterning on the undersides are useful identification features.

Humpback Whale   UPPER SIDE

North Pacific Right Whale
Very large black tail flukes with smooth edges, pointed tips and a deep central notch.

Gray Whale
Triangular tail flukes, dark gray in color with pale blotches, up to three meters wide, with a deep central notch and pointed tips.

Humpback Whale   UNDERSIDE
Large tail flukes, forming a shallow V; the trailing edges are always irregular with variable white patterning on the underside.

Blue Whale UPPER SIDE

Sperm Whale UPPER SIDE

Blue Whale UNDERSIDE
Crescent-shaped tail flukes, appearing slim compared to the very thick tail stock; upper sides dark; undersides pale with a dark border.

Sperm Whale UNDERSIDE
Tail flukes large, triangular and completely dark, with smooth edges and a deep central notch.

Surfacing sequences of the larger whales

Many of the larger whales are very similar in appearance, yet the shape and position of certain features and the manner in which they move at the surface can be quite different. Paying close attention to the surfacing sequence of the larger whales can therefore aid identification. Of particular significance in some species is the timing of the appearance of the head (or blow) in relation to the dorsal fin, and whether the tail flukes or tail stock are raised prior to a deep dive. This section shows, from left to right, the appearance of the blow, head, upper back and, for some species, the tail flukes during a typical surfacing sequence.

Common Minke Whale: *Easily the smallest of the larger whales; blow usually not visible; dorsal fin appears and disappears rapidly; tail flukes not raised.*

Humpback Whale: *Vertical, tall, bushy blow appears simultaneously with hump-shaped dorsal fin; tail flukes raised high prior to deep dive, revealing unique pattern on undersides.*

Sperm Whale: *Blow bushy, angled forward and to the left; body often motionless, appearing like a floating log; dorsal hump forms peak of triangle as body arches for a deep dive, slowly raising dark triangular tail flukes vertically above the surface.*

Sei Whale: *Tall, column-shaped blow appears at the same time as the curved dorsal fin; head and body appear dark; tail flukes not raised before a deep dive. Be aware that young Fin Whales c* *show a similar surfacing sequence.*

Bryde's Whale: *Tall, column-shaped blow appears just before curved dorsal fin; head and body appear dark; tail flukes not raised.*

Fin Whale: *Blow very tall and column-shaped; head appears first, often revealing a white lower right jaw; long back rolls forward before revealing blunt-tipped dorsal fin; tail flukes not raised. Be aware that young Fin Whale can show a similar surfacing sequence to adult Sei Whale.*

Blue Whale: Broad head appears first, with gigantic blow revealed as a robust column; "freckled" gray back rolls slowly forward, eventually revealing a tiny dorsal fin; tail flukes occasionally raised before a deep dive.

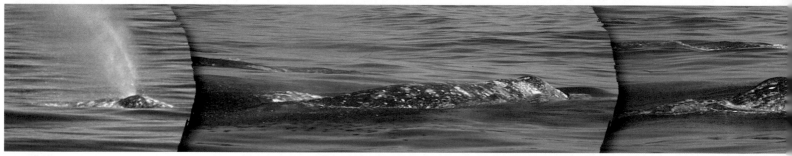

Gray Whale: Blow tall and bushy; speckled gray back rolls forward slowly and lacks a dorsal fin; tail flukes raised high before a deep dive.

North Pacific Right Whale: Blow bushy, often appearing V-shaped or heart-shaped; head covered in pale callosities; body lies low in the water and lacks a dorsal fin. Tail flukes raised high before a deep dive.

Traveling

The distances that marine mammals travel are largely dictated by the availability of their prey. The distribution of prey tends to be patchy, and varies with the seasons, shifting ocean currents and changes in water temperature. Although some marine mammals have populations that are resident and remain faithful to a home range, most cover vast distances. Some dolphins spend up to 55% of each day on the move, while several rorqual whales are capable of traveling at over 15 mph (25 km/h) for several hours.

During their extensive oceanic travels, marine mammals employ a number of techniques to conserve energy. As air creates less drag than water, many dolphins and sea lions are capable of increasing their speed during fast travel by frequently lifting their bodies clear of the water. This is known as "running" or "porpoising," although this is a misleading term as porpoises do not engage in this behavior! Large groups of dolphins engaged in porpoising is an extremely impressive sight.

Marine mammals can also move very rapidly without lifting their bodies clear of the water. Some dolphins and porpoises are capable of swimming so quickly at the surface that their bodies push water away from them, creating a splash known as a "rooster tail." Another bizarre surfacing activity is termed "skimming," and involves swimming rapidly with the head held above the surface.

Usually, though, marine mammals travel at a leisurely pace, showing only their upper bodies as they surface. This is known as slow travel. Occasionally in cetaceans even the body is obscured and only the dorsal fin betrays the presence of the animal at the surface in a behavior called "sharking." Pods of dolphins tend to move in a highly coordinated manner, often changing course as a single unit. This is most apparent when they travel line-abreast in a formation known as a "chorus line." Chorus lines may involve anything from a few animals traveling side by side to tens or hundreds of individuals strung out over a mile or more. Short-finned Pilot Whales are particularly noted for forming very long chorus lines.

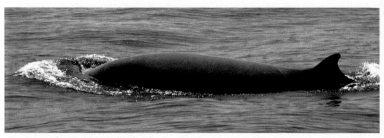

Slow travel (Cuvier's Beaked Whale): *The directional movement of a marine mammal traveling steadily while only raising the upperparts of its body as it surfaces.*

Fast travel (Blue Whales): *The directional movement of a marine mammal traveling rapidly while only raising the upperparts of its body as it surfaces.*

Porpoising or running (Fraser's Dolphins): *Very fast movement involving arc-shaped leaps clear of the water with a clean headfirst re-entry. This behavior is generally restricted to some dolphin and pinniped species.*

Sharking (Risso's Dolphin): *Swimming just beneath the surface so that only the dorsal fin shows. This behavior is frequently observed in dolphins and some whales, including surface-feeding Sei Whales.*

Skimming (Rough-toothed Dolphin): *Swimming at high speed with the head and chin above the surface of the water. This peculiar behavior is unique to Rough-toothed Dolphins.*

Rooster tail (Dall's Porpoise): *The spray of water shaped like a rooster's tail, which occurs when some robust cetaceans move rapidly at the surface without raising their bodies clear of the water. Rooster tails are a specialty of the Dall's Porpoise.*

Chorus line (Risso's Dolphins): *The coordinated movement of a group of marine mammals as they surface in a line abreast. This behavior is frequently observed in members of the blackfish family and the Risso's Dolphin, often when they are searching for prey.*

Wave riding

Marine mammals, especially dolphins, often ride waves. As yet the reasons for this are not fully understood, although it is suspected that, like surfers on the beach, they do it for the sheer fun of it. The most commonly observed method of wave riding is bow riding, the act of swimming in the pressure wave created by the bow of a moving boat or ship. The wave propels the body upward and forward, and often no propulsion is required by the animal to ride ahead of the bow. In fact, dolphins were probably bow riding long before boats existed, since thay can sometimes be seen riding the pressure wave created by a large whale as it surfaces. In addition to bow riding, many small cetaceans also enjoy riding in the wake of passing vessels and even in the surf just before it crashes onto the beach. Killer Whales and Steller Sea Lions have even been known to intentionally surf onto the shore in surprise attacks on unsuspecting pinniped pups.

Surfing the waves can allow a cetacean to increase its swimming speed significantly. The Short-beaked Common Dolphin, which may be the fastest cetacean of all, is capable of traveling at 28 mph (45 km/h) in open water, and has been recorded at speeds of 37 mph (59 km/h) while riding a ship's bow wave.

The desire to bow ride often leads dolphins to travel some distance in order to hitch a ride. Consequently, they often appear at the bow without warning and stay with the vessel for a considerable time. On a small boat, it may be possible to listen to the whistles and squeaks of bow riding dolphins as they socialize with each other. Some of the species of cetacean that regularly bow ride in the North American Pacific are illustrated on the following pages.

Bow riding (Common Bottlenose Dolphins): *Swimming in the pressure wave created ahead of large objects pushing through the water such as whales or ships. This behavior, a specialty of most dolphins, is useful in assisting with identification as some species and populations are more keen to ride the bow than others.*

Wake riding (Pacific White-sided Dolphins): *Some species of dolphin, including striped and Pacific White-sided Dolphin, often show a preference for riding on waves created in the wake of a vessel.*

Surf riding (Common Bottlenose Dolphins): *Like surfers, dolphins and some whales enjoy riding the lee slopes of oceanic waves or the tops of breaking waves in the surf.*

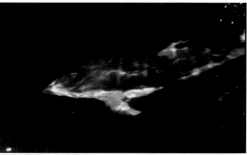

Bow riding (Pacific White-sided Dolphin)

Bow riding (Short-beaked Common Dolphins)

Bow riding (Striped Dolphin)

Bow riding (Northern Right Whale Dolphins)

Bow riding (Dall's Porpoise)

Bow riding (Melon-headed Whales)

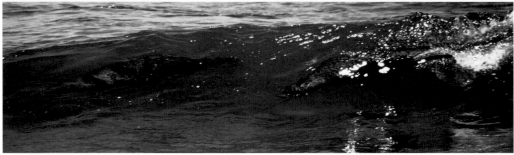

Surf riding (California Sea Lions)

Bow riding (False Killer Whales)

Resting

Marine mammals like to feel the sun on their backs almost as much as people do. Pinnipeds enjoy hauling out of the water to bask on a beach or on the rocks but this is generally avoided by Sea Otters and is not an option for cetaceans. Instead they lie motionless at the surface, often giving the appearance of floating logs. This is known as logging or rafting. Logging is not restricted to sunny days as it may also indicate that a marine mammal is asleep, resting or recuperating between dives. In the case of pinnipeds, rafting often involves raising the flippers clear of the water. This strange-looking behavior, known as jugging, is a means of regulating body temperature (thermoregulation).

Jugging (California Sea Lion): *The appearance of sea lions or fur seals resting at the surface with both hind limbs and one fore limb exposed to conserve heat. The term derives from the fact that their bodies are held in a position reminiscent of a jug handle.*

Hauling out (Harbor Seals): *The act of leaving the water at a suitable location in order to rest or molt. Such a location is known as a haulout. Pinnipeds haul out together to breed, rest, avoid predators, molt and warm themselves.*

Logging or rafting (Sea Otter): *Resting motionless at the water's surface in a horizontal position.*

Logging or rafting (Short-finned Pilot Whales)

Surface feeding

Marine mammals employ a remarkable variety of hunting techniques in order to catch the diverse range of prey species they pursue, and many of these techniques take place or culminate at the sea surface.

There are two strikingly different tactics employed by marine mammals during feeding. First, there are the filter-feeders. Baleen whales have evolved to be filter-feeders, specializing in engulfing enormous quantities of small fish or crustaceans at the times of year when populations of such prey are at their densest. By engulfing seawater and prey in one maneuver, baleen whales filter water from their mouths through a series of comb-like baleen plates hanging from both sides of the upper jaw, before swallowing the bounty left high and dry on the tongue. The number and size of baleen plates are unique to each species.

In order to make the most of the ocean's harvest, baleen whales have become the largest animals to have ever lived on Earth. Right Whales have developed enormous arched jaws, from which hang the longest baleen plates of all at up to 8.9 feet (2.7 m). These whales specialize in skim feeding and, as they move slowly forward with their mouths wide open, millions of tiny crustaceans are trapped inside the jaws before the water is strained out.

The rorqual whales have adapted their filter-feeding still further, as their throats are made up of many pleated grooves (folded skin) that expand like an enormous balloon to increase the volume of water that can be held. Rorqual whales can also disarticulate the lower jaw from the upper jaw in order to increase the area of the gape.

The toothed cetaceans, pinnipeds and Sea Otters employ a more conventional mammalian method of hunting by tracking down and grasping relatively large individual prey items in their jaws. This adaptable method has enabled them to exploit a great variety of prey at higher levels of the food chain. If their diet includes hard-bodied prey such as fish, the jaw is generally lined with teeth. However, some species feed predominantly on soft-bodied prey such as squid, and no longer require teeth for gripping their quarry. These species often have relatively few teeth, and in some cases teeth are completely absent.

Marine mammals use a variety of methods to locate their prey, including vision, hearing and the detection of tiny vibrations through whiskers. The toothed cetaceans are probably the best equipped of all marine mammals in terms of foraging adaptations as they possess sonar, the ability to build up a picture of their surroundings by emitting a sound and using the information received from the returning echo (echolocation). This enables toothed cetaceans to find food at great depth, at night and in waters that are turbid or cloudy. Cetaceans with sonar are even capable of pinpointing flatfish buried in the sand.

Marine mammals are incredibly successful ocean feeders having adapted to hunt at most depths, throughout all of the oceans, seas and some rivers from the tropics to the poles. They employ a staggering range of techniques to seek out, trap and secure their prey. These techniques range from Humpback Whales releasing bubbles to trap schooling Capelin, Killer Whales stunning herring by whacking them with their tail flukes and Sea Otters using stones as tools to crack clams. This section details all of the regularly observed surface feeding maneuvers with the exception of two methods regularly used by cetaceans to stun prey, particularly schooling fish: tail slapping and breaching. These techniques are covered elsewhere because they are also displayed for reasons not associated with feeding and therefore merit inclusion under their own headings (see pages 51–57).

Lunge feeding (Blue Whale): *The expanded throat grooves of rorqual whales.*

Skim feeding (North Pacific Right Whale): *Showing the tips of the baleen plates.*

Lunge feeding (Common Minke Whale): *The explosive movement of a whale as it rises clear of the water with its jaws wide open to catch large schools of fish or invertebrates. When executing this maneuver the whale's head and body is thrust vertically upward into the air. The jaw is opened wide as the whale breaks the surface but closes quickly afterwards. Fish can often be seen leaping from the gaping jaws. Lunges can occur at all angles with the whale resubmerging as it crashes down on its back, side or belly. Alternatively, the whale may slip quietly below the surface while in the vertical position. Lunge feeding is particularly characteristic of the rorqual whales. Their expanded throat grooves may be flushed pink with exertion as the whale takes in a large volume of prey and seawater simultaneously. Unlike breaching, only the head and upper body leave the water during a lunge.*

Skim feeding (Gray Whale): *Several baleen whales regularly skim the surface with their mouths wide open to catch prey. The surface of the water acts as a barrier so that schooling fish and invertebrates have less chance of escape. Some whales, particularly Fin Whales, often skim feed on their sides with half of their tail flukes visible above the surface. Sudden turns to the left or right are often made while skim feeding, particularly by the Sei Whale.*

Echelon feeding (Humpback Whales): The coordinated movement of a group of whales as they feed side by side with jaws wide open.

Bubble netting (Humpback Whales): A cooperative method employed by some species of cetacean and pinniped to catch large schools of fish or invertebrates by trapping them inside walls, columns or clouds of bubbles created by releasing air. Schooling fish flee from bubbles released by the marine mammals below, and are reluctant to cross them. Bubble netting usually involves several animals working as a coordinated unit, pushing the prey to the surface where they become trapped. Humpback Whales are famous for using this technique but it is now known from several other species.

NOT ILLUSTRATED

Prey herding: The coordinated movement of a group of marine mammals as they take advantage of the instinctive schooling behavior of their prey. Individuals herd the prey in an encircling maneuver, often pushing them to the surface. The shoal forms a tight ball as fish become confused and unable to escape. Finally the predators attack, with individuals swimming into the middle of the circle while others maintain the "net" by continuing to swim in circles. This hunting strategy has been reported for many species of dolphin, sea lion and porpoise, and is often associated with exuberant surface activity such as tail slapping and breaching, which causes the prey schools to further compact in fright.

Fish whacking: The tail of a cetacean is a powerful weapon which is sometimes used for hunting. Common Bottlenose Dolphins sometimes whack fish into the air, and Killer Whales are capable of lifting porpoises and pinnipeds out of the water with a sweep of the tail flukes.

Tool usage (Sea Otter): Although the constructive use of an implement has been recorded in some dolphins, by far the most famous marine mammal tool-user is the Sea Otter. Sea Otters regularly use rocks to crush the shells of mussels, crabs and sea urchins. Often using a favorite stone many times, Sea Otters will rise to the surface and place the stone on their bellies before using it like an anvil to break open shellfish. Stones are also used to smash abalone off rocks.

Breaching

Breaching, the act of propelling the body upward until at least 40% of it is clear of the water, is one of the most spectacular sights in nature and, in the case of whales, is generally the only opportunity that most whale-watchers get to see the entire animal.

Most cetaceans are capable of breaching, with the exception of adult Blue Whales, which are quite simply too heavy. Some species breach only rarely, while others breach regularly throughout the year, at certain seasons or in certain locations. In some areas, breaching is more regularly performed by calves, or by one sex more than the other. Breaches by one animal also sometimes appear to trigger breaches by others in the same area.

Cetaceans conduct several different types of breach. Depending on the size, weight and behavior of the animal, breaches may be fast or slow. Sometimes, in the case of the larger whales, the breach can seem like it is taking place in slow motion, with the animal typically raising around 90% of its body clear of the surface, twisting, then crashing down on the water in a torrent of spray. This spray is sometimes visible from several miles away. Unlike the large whales, some medium-sized whales and almost all of the dolphins are capable of acrobatic leaps and somersaults, rising high above the water and twisting or spinning before crashing down or returning to the water with a clean entry. Although breaches angled forward or backward sometimes occur, most cetaceans rise vertically from the water before landing on their side, back or belly. Multiple breaches involving several leaps in quick succession are commonly observed in many species, and usually involve animals breaching highest during the early part of the sequence before showing less of their bodies above the water as they tire.

Breaching differs from lunging, in which prey are engulfed as the animal leaves the water with its jaws wide open; and from porpoising, in which the animal returns to the water with minimum resistance while traveling. It is not known precisely why cetaceans breach, but there may be several reasons. These include display, annoyance, aggression, a show of strength, a means of stunning or herding prey, a method of shedding parasites from the skin, a way of signaling to nearby animals, or inhaling water-free air in rough seas—or, perhaps, for fun.

Breaching (Killer Whale)

Gray Whale

Fin Whale

Sperm Whale

North Pacific Right Whale

Humpback Whale

Cuvier's Beaked Whale

Blainville's Beaked Whale

Baird's Beaked Whale

False Killer Whale

Dwarf Sperm Whale

Striped Dolphin

Northern Right Whale Dolphin

Rough-toothed Dolphin

Risso's Dolphin

Spinning (Spinner Dolphin): *Spinning behavior involves the rotation of the body along the longitudinal axis during a breach. This is a specialty of the Spinner Dolphin, which may make as many as seven complete spins during a single leap.*

Tail-walking (Pacific White-sided Dolphin): *During tail-walking a cetacean gives the impression that it is walking on water by holding its body in a vertical position before crashing down. This behavior is regularly observed in the Northern Right Whale Dolphin.*

Somersault (Pacific White-sided Dolphin): *This acrobatic movement, a trademark of several dolphin species, involves the animal turning head over tail while clear of the water.*

Somersault (Spinner Dolphin)

Slapping

As with breaching, the reasons for slapping are not fully understood but appear to include display, aggression, communication, excitement or a means of stunning prey. The sound created by a slap is probably important for communication. By slapping parts of its body against the surface, a cetacean can make itself heard over a considerable distance. Whales, dolphins and porpoises are capable of slapping their tails, flippers, heads and even dorsal fins against the surface, but the most impressive slapping behavior involves the tail flukes. In large cetaceans, this is known as lobtailing. When small cetaceans, particularly dolphins and porpoises, flex their tails against the surface, this is called tail slapping.

Flipper slapping (Humpback Whale): *The raising of a flipper into the air before bringing it crashing down on the water surface.*

Dorsal fin slapping (Killer Whale): *By rotating the body to one side, some cetaceans, especially Killer Whales, are capable of slapping their dorsal fin against the water.*

Tail slapping (Killer Whale): *Small cetaceans, particularly dolphins, are capable of lifting their tail flukes above the water and bringing them crashing down. This behavior may be repeated many times in a single session.*

Lobtailing (Humpback Whale): *The act of a large whale lifting its tail high out of the water before slapping the flukes against the surface. This is often repeated many times.*

Head slapping (Humpback Whale): *A behavior sometimes seen in large whales, when the head is raised clear of the water and then slapped down rapidly on the surface.*

Spyhopping

Marine mammals have excellent eyesight. As visibility is almost always better above the surface than it is below, they occasionally raise their heads clear of the surface in order to have a look around. Such behavior can be extremely useful in survival situations such as locating the position of a passing vessel or looking for escape holes or channels in enclosing pack ice. During close encounters with whale-watching boats, a curious marine mammal will often spyhop to take a look at the people on board, leading to speculation as to who is really watching whom!

Killer Whales

Risso's Dolphin

Short-finned Pilot Whale

North Pacific Right Whale

Common Minke Whale

Sperm Whale

Gray Whale

Other surface maneuvers

Marine mammals regularly exhibit a number of behaviors while at the surface which do not fit into the categories listed so far in this section.

Belly up (Short-finned Pilot Whale): *A term for lying motionless in the water with the belly pointing skyward. This often occurs during bouts of social behavior and is also employed by female whales as they attempt to avoid the attentions of a male wishing to mate.*

Tail throwing (Humpback Whale): *Flinging the tail flukes violently from side to side above the water.*

Roll over (False Killer Whale): *Refers to the rotation of the body through 360° returning to an upright position.*

Headstand (Risso's Dolphin): *This behavior involves lying vertically, head-down before raising the tail flukes upward until clear of the water. Risso's Dolphins are capable of holding their flukes in this manner for up to two minutes.*

Aggregations / super-pods (Long-beaked Common Dolphins)

Flipper waving (Humpback Whale): *Some whales, particularly Humpbacks, can wave one or both flippers in the air from side to side while lying on their side or back.*

Aggregations / super-pods (Fin Whales): *When several individuals or groups of a particular species of marine mammal come together in order to hunt, mate, raise young or defend themselves against predators.*

Breeding

Marine mammals employ a wide range of breeding strategies. Many give birth to their young in early summer when food is plentiful. Others, such as the larger baleen whales and Northern Elephant Seal, spend the summer gorging themselves and building up fat reserves as blubber. In the winter, they seek "sheltered" locations to mate and give birth. They do not feed during this period and rely upon their fat reserves for energy.

The coming together of two animals to mate is a more elegant process in the water than it is on land. Male pinnipeds mount females at the rookeries, whereas cetaceans mate belly to belly. In both cases, mating is often preceded by exciteable behavior, including chasing, rolling over and fighting. Males are often left with raw or bleeding wounds or scars as a result of fights.

The gestation period in marine mammals is relatively long, lasting between 8 and 16 months. The reproductive cycle is also slow. Marine mammals generally give birth to a single offspring, which takes between six months and several years to reach independence, and several more years to reach sexual maturity. This reproductive strategy is successful because the survival rate of the offspring is high, and because adults are long-lived, with females capable of bearing many young during their lifetime.

Marine mammals are generally about a third of the length of their parents at birth. Adults and their young develop a close bond, which whalers have long exploited by deliberately harpooning calves in the knowledge that the mother, and sometimes the entire family, will stay close by. In some species, the bond between a mother and its offspring may remain for only a few months, but in others it can last for several years or even an entire lifetime.

Common Bottlenose Dolphins

Bulls fighting (Northern Elephant Seals)

Mating (Northern Elephant Seals)

Mating (Long-beaked Common Dolphins)

A pup suckling its mother (Northern Elephant Seals)

Interspecies associations

Marine mammals are highly gregarious, with mixed species groups often occurring and associations even being formed with other large predators such as tuna or seabirds. The majority of these associations form because of a requirement for food. These associations may act as a means of improving hunting efficiency, either because large numbers of predators make catching prey easier or because predators with different skills are able to hunt more efficiently in partnership. Associations may also be formed for social reasons, such as to increase protection against predators. The inquisitive nature of marine mammals has increasingly brought them into close contact with boats and people; Gray Whales on their breeding grounds may even actively seek physical contact.

Cetaceans and seals (Common Bottlenose Dolphins and California Sea Lions)

Marine mammals and people (Humpback Whale)

Dolphins and whales (Fin Whale and Short-beaked Common Dolphins)

Marine mammals and birds (Humpback Whales and Sooty Shearwaters)

Stranding

The process by which a marine mammal is cast ashore in a helpless or dead state is known as a stranding. This term is usually used in relation to cetaceans. Pinnipeds can also strand, although they regularly come ashore voluntarily. Strandings usually involve lone individuals but can sometimes involve small groups and, in extreme cases, several hundred animals. Most strandings are of dead animals that have been carried by the prevailing winds and currents before being washed ashore with the tide. Marine mammals tend to float for a while after death due to the gases of decomposition that inflate the body. Most sink eventually, but a small proportion get washed ashore.

Marine mammals are also regularly found stranded alive. This behavior has perplexed people for centuries and still remains something of an unsolved mystery. Scientists have suggested a number of possible reasons for strandings that counter the historical view that they were simply committing suicide, a theory supported by the fact that some individuals strand repeatedly, even if they have been refloated and led away from the shore.

Research has also suggested that whales may lose their navigational ability, perhaps as a result of illness or infection, or that the coastal geology or topography of some headlands and bays are more confusing to marine mammals than others, resulting in a relatively high number of strandings. It is also possible that deep-water species, which occasionally enter shallow water in search of prey, may be more prone to stranding than species which frequent coastal waters and are therefore used to navigating in the shallows.

Some species strand more frequently and in greater numbers than others. This may be due to the strong family bonds that exist in some species. Certain toothed whales, such as Short-finned Pilot Whales, False Killer Whales and Sperm Whales are particularly vulnerable to coming ashore in numbers in a phenomenon known as mass stranding. These animals live in family groups and rely on each other for survival. When one animal becomes ill or is injured, others within the group, many of which may be related to the ailing animal, remain with it even if it seeks refuge in shallow water to rest or is too weak to swim and gets washed near shore by the tide. Eventually the animal may strand with family members remaining alongside and sharing in the same fate.

It is likely that a number of factors may lead to a marine mammal stranding. Whatever the reason, there can be no doubt that these events have enabled scientists to learn much about the ecology and biology of marine mammals, many of which remain poorly studied at sea. Research into strandings continues today through schemes that enable beached animals to be reported so that they can be analyzed for signs of injury or ill health as a result of factors such as entanglement in fishing gear, collisions with vessels or pollution.

A stranded Cuvier's Beaked Whale

Marine mammal families

A total of 46 species of marine mammals has been recorded in the North American Pacific. All marine mammals belong to the orders Cetacea or Carnivora, which can be further divided into 11 groups (which are broadly equivalent to families). This section aims to provide a brief overview of the key features that identify these groups, along with some background information on their historical status and distribution.

CETACEAN FAMILIES

Whales, dolphins and porpoises belong to the order Cetacea, collectively known as cetaceans. The order Cetacea consists of more than 80 species, and is divided into two suborders: the Mysticeti or baleen whales; and the Odontoceti or toothed cetaceans. The odontocetes exhibit a much greater diversity than the mysticetes, with over 70 classified species. There are two major differences in the physical structure of these two groups. Mysticetes have two blowholes and have plates of baleen (whalebone) hanging from the roof of the mouth; odontocetes have a single nostril or blowhole and possess teeth. Additionally, the toothed cetaceans, which hunt agile fish and squid, locate their prey using sonar while baleen whales have not yet been shown to use echolocation and may instead rely on sight to locate the large shoals of fish and krill upon which they feed.

There is considerable debate about the precise number of species in the order Cetacea, and in the last two decades several new species of whale have been discovered. It is likely that recent advances in genetic analysis will lead to the discovery of further species or the reclassification of existing ones.

The 39 cetacean species that have been recorded in the North American Pacific can be divided into the following eight groups.

RIGHT and BOWHEAD WHALES — *Family: Balaenidae*

North Pacific Right Whale (page 76)

This family comprises three species of Right Whale and the Bowhead Whale. Like the rorquals (Balaenopteridae), Right and Bowhead Whales are generally large, have a distinctive tall blow, and capture vast amounts of prey by filter-feeding. However, they differ from the rorquals in several respects: they have a strongly arched rostrum, which in profile forms a deeply curved jawline (in contrast to the near-straight line of a rorqual jaw); the throat grooves cannot be extended to take in more water (although the baleen plates, longer and more slender than those of a rorqual, increase the filtering capacity to compensate); and they lack a dorsal fin. They are also exceptionally bulky compared with the rorquals.

The North Pacific Right Whale is the only member of the Balaenidae to occur in the North American Pacific. Along with the North Atlantic Right Whale this was one of the first species of whale to be hunted. It was so called because it was the "Right Whale" to hunt—it swam slowly, came close to shore frequently, remained afloat after it was killed and had a high yield of baleen and oil. No other group

North Pacific Right Whale

Gray Whale

of whales was hunted to such precariously low levels. Despite many decades of protection, both the North Atlantic and North Pacific Right Whales still number only a few hundred individuals and remain perilously close to extinction.

GRAY WHALE — *Family: Eschrichtiidae*

Gray Whale (page 78)

The Gray Whale is the sole member of the family Eschrichtiidae. Gray Whales are somewhat intermediate in appearance between Right Whales (Balaenidae) and rorquals (Balaenopteridae). Gray Whales have short, narrow heads, a slightly arched rostrum and between two and five longitudinal grooves on the throat (instead of the balaenopterid ventral pleats). The baleen is yellowish-white and is much heavier and shorter than in other mysticetes. Unlike the rorquals, Gray Whales lack a dorsal fin, but do have a dorsal ridge of 6 to 12 small humps along the last third of the back.

Gray Whales are the most coastal of the mysticetes and are frequently found within a few miles of the shore. This species was intensively hunted throughout its range, but the population in the North American Pacific has made an excellent recovery since hunting was banned and is now estimated to have reached pre-exploitation levels.

RORQUAL WHALES — *Family: Balaenopteridae*

Humpback Whale (page 82)
Blue Whale (page 86)
Fin Whale (page 88)
Sei Whale (page 90)
Bryde's Whale (page 92)
Common Minke Whale (page 94)

With the exception of the Common Minke Whale, all rorqual whales occurring in the North American Pacific are large to very large. Within this group of whales is the largest animal ever to have lived on the planet: the giant Blue Whale, which can reach a length of 98 feet (30 m) and weigh over 154 tons (140 metric tonnes). Sadly, most of the larger species were hunted intensively during the last century, and their numbers have been severely reduced. Following the international ban on whaling in 1986, several populations have shown signs of slow recovery, but many still remain depleted.

Rorquals have several features that distinguish them from other groups. The name "rorqual" is derived from the Norwegian language and literally means "furrow whale"—a reference to the series of throat grooves that extend underneath the lower jaw. Rorquals do not possess teeth, but instead have a series of comblike structures called baleen plates that hang from the upper jaw. They feed by opening their cavernous jaws as they swim along, and expanding their throat grooves, vastly increasing the volume of water held within their mouth. When the mouth is closed, water is sieved through the baleen plates leaving quantities of small fish and zooplankton trapped inside.

Despite their enormous size, rorquals are sleek and streamlined and capable of considerable speed. They have large, flattened heads with a centrally located twin blowhole. The dorsal fin is set far back on the body toward the tail. The tail flukes are large and broad. Several members of this group travel great distances between their cold-water summer feeding grounds and warm-water winter breeding grounds, though other rorquals, such as Bryde's Whale, show little evidence of predictable seasonal movements. Of the eight known species of rorqual, six occur in the North American Pacific.

SPERM WHALES *Families: Physeteridae and Kogidae*

Sperm Whale (page 96) *Dwarf Sperm Whale (page 100)*
Pygmy Sperm Whale (page 98)

Sperm Whales get their name from an unusual shared characteristic: spermaceti, a semi-liquid waxy oil that fills the spermaceti organ in their enlarged heads. The function of this strange fluid is the subject of some debate, but it is thought either to be an aid to buoyancy control or to act as an acoustic lens to focus sound during echolocation.

Although Sperm Whales include the largest and the smallest toothed whales from two different families, their basic body shapes are quite similar. All three species share a large, squarish head, a long underslung jaw with uniform teeth, paddle-shaped flippers and a single blowhole that is positioned slightly to the left of the top of the head.

The Sperm Whale is the largest of the toothed whales and makes possibly the deepest and longest dives of any creature in the animal kingdom—they have been accurately recorded by sonar diving to 3,930 feet (1,200 m), and may reach even greater depths. The Sperm Whale's head is particularly massive, comprising up to one-third of its overall length.

Fin Whale

Sperm Whale

In the Pygmy and Dwarf Sperm Whales, the head is more conical and much shorter in relation to the overall body length. They are rather shark-like in appearance with thin, very sharp, curved teeth. They also have a bracket-shaped mark on the side of the head resembling the gill of a fish. These are cryptic animals and are very undemonstrative.

BEAKED WHALES	Family: Ziphiidae
Cuvier's Beaked Whale (page 104)	Hubbs' Beaked Whale (page 113)
Baird's Beaked Whale (page 106)	Ginkgo-toothed Beaked Whale (page 114)
Longman's Beaked Whale (page 108)	Perrin's Beaked Whale (page 115)
Blainville's Beaked Whale (page 110)	Pygmy Beaked Whale (page 116)
Stejneger's Beaked Whale (page 112)	

The family name Ziphiidae comes from the distinctive, protruding jaw or beak that is found in all species; it is derived from the Greek word *xiphos*, meaning sword—hence Ziphiidae, or "sword-nosed" whale. These medium-sized whales have a relatively small dorsal fin that is situated two-thirds of the way along the back toward the tail. The tail flukes are proportionally large and usually lack a central notch. Most species have retained only a single pair of teeth that protrude

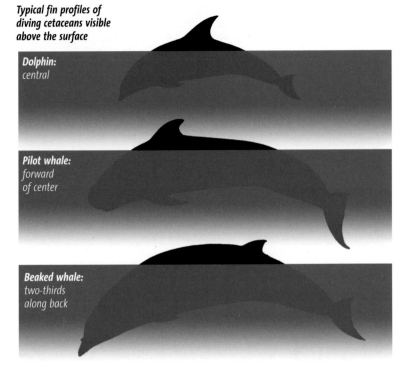

Typical fin profiles of diving cetaceans visible above the surface

Dolphin: central

Pilot whale: forward of center

Beaked whale: two-thirds along back

Cuvier's Beaked Whale

from the closed mouths in adults to form tusks. In all but the genus *Berardius* these tusks only erupt above the gumline in adult males. The tusks appear to be used as weapons, and in most species mature males are heavily scarred with tusk rakes.

Due to their similar body shapes and coloration, most beaked whales, particularly those in the genus *Mesoplodon* are notoriously difficult to identify. The main difference between the species in this genus is the position of protruding teeth—which needs to be seen, and ideally photographed, in order to confirm identification.

Nine of the 20 species of beaked whale found throughout the world are known to occur in the North American Pacific. However, because of their deep-water habits and unobtrusive behavior almost nothing is known about any of them. Three new species of beaked whale have been described in the last 15 years, reflecting the enormous amount still to be learned about the distribution, ecology and identification of this mysterious family.

BLACKFISH — Family: *Delphinidae*

Killer Whale (or Orca) (page 120)

Pygmy Killer Whale (page 128)

Short-finned Pilot Whale (page 124)

Melon-headed Whale (page 130)

False Killer Whale (page 126)

Blackfish include the largest members of the dolphin family, but each species is named as a whale because the majority of the group attains a similar size to the beaked and other medium-sized whales. However, two members of the group are actually no bigger than the "typical" dolphin species. As the name suggests, they are predominantly black in color. All members of this group lack a noticeable beak and have a relatively large, prominent dorsal fin. Like other dolphins, blackfish are highly social animals, often living their lives in discrete family groups. They are efficient pack-hunters, capable of considerable speed, and exhibit a range of interesting behaviors such as spyhopping, tail slapping and breaching. The Killer Whale is a well-known predator of other mammals, including the largest whales. The False Killer Whale, and Pygmy Killer Whale, and both long-finned and Short-finned Pilot Whales have also been observed to be aggressive toward other cetaceans. Five of the six species of blackfish found throughout the world occur in the North American Pacific.

DOLPHINS — Family: *Delphinidae*

Risso's Dolphin (page 134)

Fraser's Dolphin (page 146)

Common Bottlenose Dolphin (page 136)

Short-beaked Common Dolphin (page 148)

Rough-toothed Dolphin (page 138)

Long-beaked Common Dolphin (page 150)

Spinner Dolphin (page 140)

Pacific White-sided Dolphin (page 152)

Pantropical Spotted Dolphin (page 142)

Northern Right Whale Dolphin (page 154)

Striped Dolphin (page 144)

Short-finned Pilot Whale

Short-beaked Common Dolphin

Dolphins are smaller than most whale species, have slim, streamlined bodies and, in most cases, tall, prominent and centrally placed dorsal fins. Their bodies show a wide variety of patterns and colors, which often provide the key to their identification. The heads of most species taper gently to a prominent beak that contains many sharp, conical teeth. They are generally social animals, often occurring in large groups and capable of great speed and spectacular acrobatics. They prey on a wide variety of squid, fish and other marine life. Of the 35 species of dolphin found throughout the world, 11 occur in the North American Pacific.

PORPOISES
Family: Phocoenidae

Dall's Porpoise (page 156) *Vaquita (page 160)*
Harbor Porpoise (page 158)

Porpoises are the smallest of all cetaceans with no member of the family exceeding 8 feet (2.5 m) in length. Unlike most dolphins, they lack a prominent beak and most have a small, triangular dorsal fin. Their teeth are laterally compressed or spade-shaped (in contrast to the conical teeth of dolphins). In general, porpoises are shy, unobtrusive animals rarely performing the kinds of acrobatics associated with dolphins. They can be difficult to see except in the calmest conditions, and only the Dall's Porpoise is readily attracted to moving vessels. Unfortunately, their preference for shallow, nearshore waters has led to pressure on many coastal populations through overfishing, accidental capture in fishing nets, and pollution. This has caused significant declines in the populations of several species, to the extent that they are currently considered threatened. Three of the six species of porpoise found throughout the world occur in the North American Pacific.

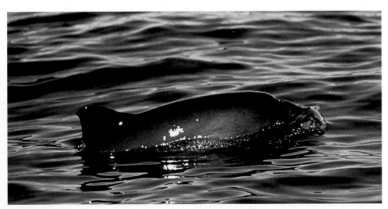

Harbor Porpoise

SEALS AND SEA LIONS (PINNIPEDS)

Pinnipeds are aquatic relatives of terrestrial mammals belonging to the order Carnivora. The term pinniped is derived from the Latin *pinnipes* meaning "web-footed," or "fin-footed." Pinnipeds are divided into three families, two of which occur in the North American Pacific: the Otariidae or eared seals, and the Phocidae or earless seals.

EARED SEALS (Fur Seals & Sea Lions)
Family: Otariidae

Northern Fur Seal (page 164) *Steller Sea Lion (page 168)*
Guadalupe Fur Seal (page 166) *California Sea Lion (page 170)*

The eared seals or otariids differ from all other pinnipeds in that they possess external ear flaps. Their pelage (fur) is generally thicker than that of the earless seals, and is made up of numerous long guard hairs overlying a thick, woolly underfur. A major difference between the eared seals and earless seals is how they move on land and in the sea. Eared seals are capable of rotating their hind flippers forward

California Sea Lion

and under their bodies enabling them to walk or run using all four limbs. In water, propulsion is provided by the fore flippers only, while the hind flippers trail behind and are used for steering. Eared seals are fast, graceful swimmers and can "porpoise" like dolphins. They are typically divided into two subgroups: sea lions and fur seals. Most sea lions are larger than fur seals, and have blunter muzzles (those of fur seals tend to be pointed). The flippers of sea lions are usually proportionately shorter than those of fur seals. They can also be identified by the layer of underfur, which is abundant in fur seals and sparse in sea lions. Four of the 14 species of eared seals found throughout the world occur in the North American Pacific.

EARLESS (TRUE) SEALS — *Family: Phocidae*

Northern Elephant Seal (page 172)   *Harbor Seal (page 174)*

The phocids are called earless or true seals because they lack external ear-flaps. Unlike eared seals, the earless seals cannot rotate their hind flippers under their bodies to walk. On land they use their fore flippers to pull them-

selves forward, while their hind flippers are dragged passively behind. In water, earless seals use their hind flippers for propulsion, with the fore flippers used primarily for steering. Earless seals have lost much of their hair and have a thicker layer of blubber than eared seals. Compared to eared seals, earless seals generally spend more time at sea, swim more slowly, and dive to deeper depths for longer periods. Of the 18 species found throughout the world, only two occur in the North American Pacific.

Northern Elephant Seal

MUSTELIDS

Like pinnipeds, Sea Otters belong to the order Carnivora, but are part of the large family Mustelidae that includes weasels, skunks and polecats. Most members of this family have long, slender bodies and short legs, rounded ears and anal scent glands. While many mustelids may be partially aquatic, only Sea Otters and marine otters live exclusively in marine waters, and of these only the Sea Otter is found in the North American Pacific.

SEA OTTERS — *Family: Mustelidae*

Sea Otter (page 176)

Sea Otters are the smallest fully aquatic mammal occurring in the North American Pacific. Unlike cetaceans and pinnipeds they lack a layer of blubber, but instead have a luxurious pelage with extremely dense fur. To ensure its fur coat is kept in prime condition the Sea Otter spends a considerable amount of time each day grooming—a behavioral "hallmark" of this species. Sea Otters, unlike all other carnivores, have blunt teeth that enable them to crush their invertebrate prey, many of which have strong exoskeletons.

Sea Otter

How to use the species accounts

In the Species accounts that follow, photographs and text are designed to allow rapid comparison between similar species. The pictures show a range of typical at-sea postures for each species, accompanied by an illustration of the complete animal and a species map showing seasonal distribution.

SPECIES MAPS

Each species account has a map showing seasonal distribution and other key information such as "hot spots" where the species is particulary abundant, breeding colonies and notable stranding records. Although these maps show "typical" seasonal distributions based on our current knowledge, the unpredictability of marine mammal movements and our limited understanding of the distribution of some species means that they should not be used in isolation to conclude a species' identification.

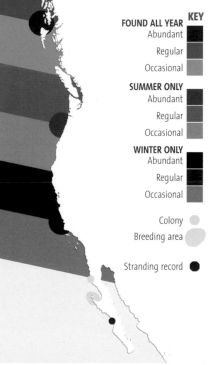

KEY

FOUND ALL YEAR
Abundant
Regular
Occasional

SUMMER ONLY
Abundant
Regular
Occasional

WINTER ONLY
Abundant
Regular
Occasional

Colony
Breeding area

Stranding record

SPECIES ACCOUNTS

The text of the species accounts is laid out as follows:

Common Name

Scientific name

Short introduction to the species.

IDENTIFICATION: A summary of the key identification features and a brief description of the most noticeable characteristics of the species.

SIMILAR SPECIES: A detailed summary of the differences to look for between confusion species to enable a confident identification.

BEHAVIOR: A description of the typical activities of the species.

STATUS AND DISTRIBUTION: A summary of summer and winter distribution, habitat preferences and migration routes together with an indication of abundance and, where appropriate, the conservation status of each species.

> Text in the tinted box gives a concise overview of the species characteristics covering, where appropriate, length, group size and notable behavior.

SCALE

Below the tinted box is an indicator of the scale of the complete animal illustration.

QUICK REFERENCE GUIDE
Baleen and
Sperm Whales

Scale 1:100

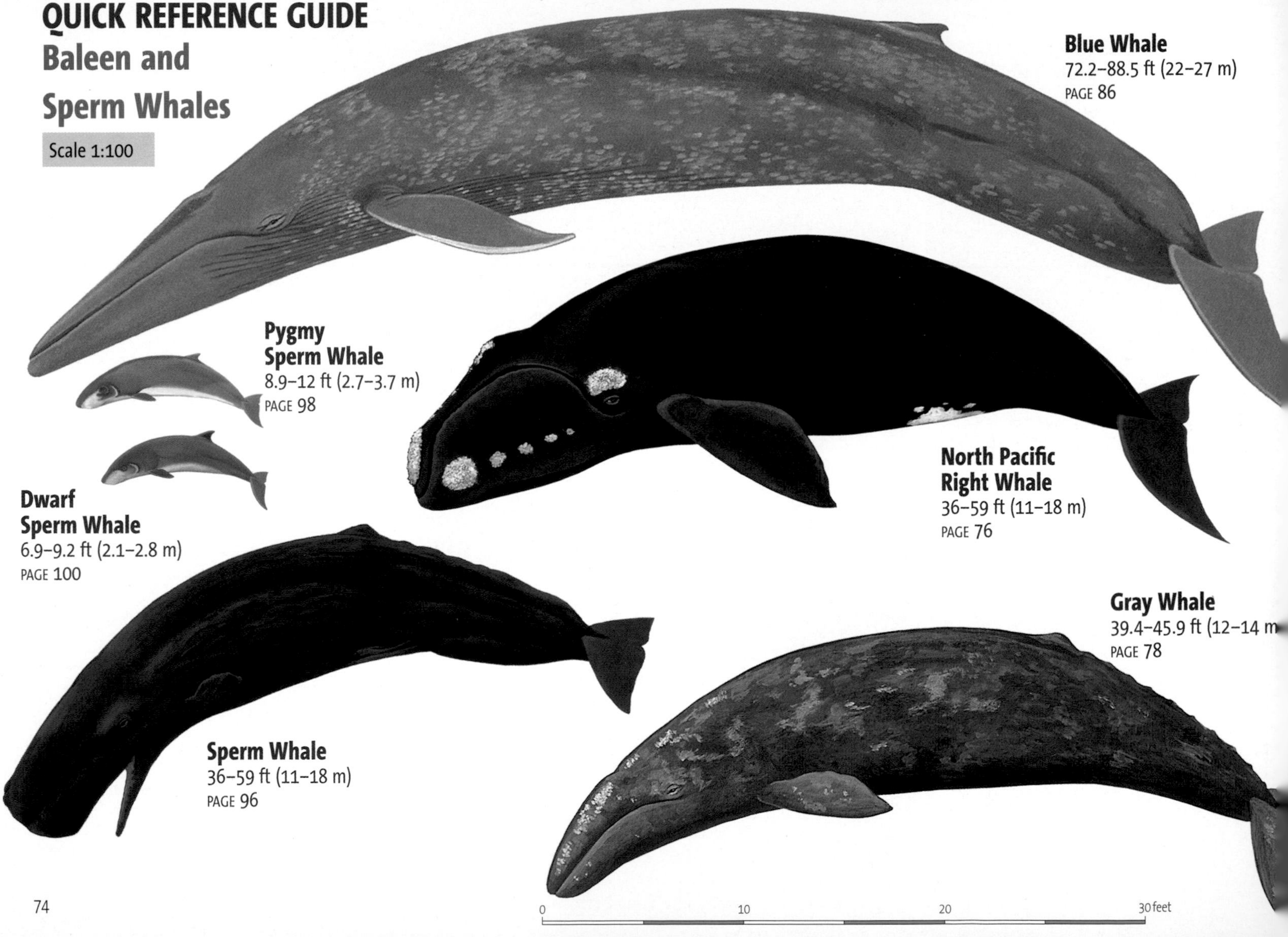

Blue Whale
72.2–88.5 ft (22–27 m)
PAGE 86

**Pygmy
Sperm Whale**
8.9–12 ft (2.7–3.7 m)
PAGE 98

**Dwarf
Sperm Whale**
6.9–9.2 ft (2.1–2.8 m)
PAGE 100

**North Pacific
Right Whale**
36–59 ft (11–18 m)
PAGE 76

Gray Whale
39.4–45.9 ft (12–14 m
PAGE 78

Sperm Whale
36–59 ft (11–18 m)
PAGE 96

0   10   20   30 feet

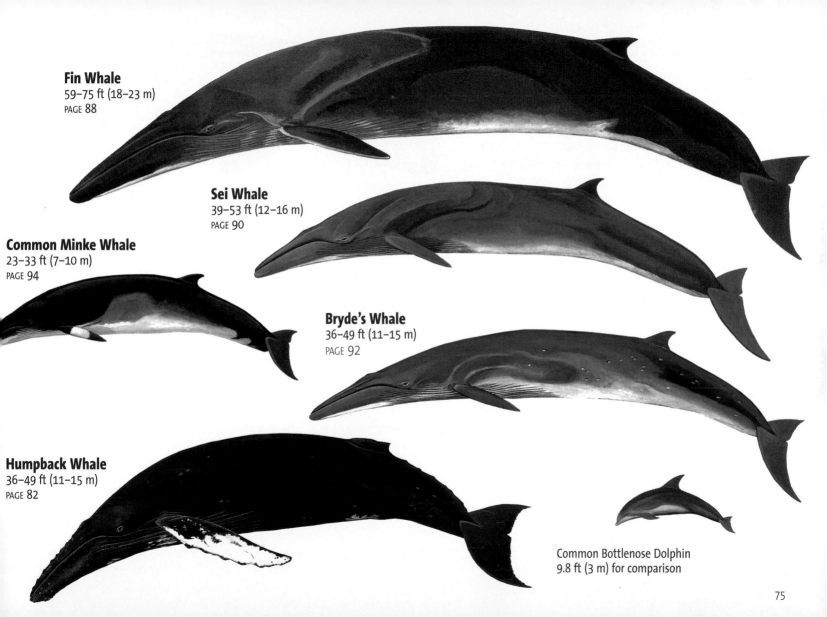

Fin Whale
59–75 ft (18–23 m)
PAGE 88

Sei Whale
39–53 ft (12–16 m)
PAGE 90

Common Minke Whale
23–33 ft (7–10 m)
PAGE 94

Bryde's Whale
36–49 ft (11–15 m)
PAGE 92

Humpback Whale
36–49 ft (11–15 m)
PAGE 82

Common Bottlenose Dolphin
9.8 ft (3 m) for comparison

North Pacific Right Whale
Eubalaena japonica

The rarest great whale in the world. Due to the rarity of the North Pacific Right Whale, the plate opposite shows images of the North Atlantic Right Whale. These two species are extremely similar and are probably indistinguishable at sea.

IDENTIFICATION: The North Pacific Right Whale is strikingly different from the other large whales of the region. The first clue to its presence is usually its distinctive blow, which is V-shaped when viewed from the front or rear. The body is large and rotund and lacks a dorsal fin. It has a proportionately large head, comprising almost one-quarter of its total length, and strongly arched jaws. Much of the head, particularly around the eyes, upper jawline and rostrum, is covered in light-colored patches known as callosities. The tail flukes, which are often raised prior to a deep dive, are very large with smooth edges, pointed tips and a deep central notch. This species is predominantly black, with small, irregular white patches on its underside.

SIMILAR SPECIES: Most likely to be confused with the Gray Whale (page 78), the North Pacific Right Whale has smooth black skin and a V-shaped blow, whereas the Gray Whale usually has a bushy blow, is gray, and is covered in barnacles. Confusion is also possible with other large whales, such as the Humpback Whale (page 82), which can sometimes appear to have a V-shaped blow, but the distinctive blow, in combination with the lack of a dorsal fin, should distinguish the North Pacific Right Whale from all other species.

BEHAVIOR: North Pacific Right Whales are slow swimmers and can be inquisitive and approachable, exhibiting a range of behaviors such as lobtailing, flipper waving and breaching. They have been observed spyhopping and raising their tail flukes vertically above the surface for prolonged periods.

STATUS AND DISTRIBUTION: The North Pacific Right Whale is restricted to warm temperate to subpolar waters of the North Pacific. This species was very heavily exploited by whalers and, along with its close relative the North Atlantic Right Whale, remains one of the world's most endangered whales. In the whole of the eastern North Pacific there have only been about 30 reliable sightings in the last century, most of which have occurred in Bristol Bay in the eastern Bering Sea. The migratory patterns of the North Pacific Right Whale are unknown, although in other oceans Right Whales generally spend the summer in high latitude feeding grounds and migrate to more temperate waters during the winter to mate and calve. Whaling records indicate that North Pacific Right Whales ranged across the entire North American Pacific, from the Gulf of Alaska south to coastal waters off central Mexico, with a pre-exploitation population in excess of 11,000 animals.

Adult length: 36–59 ft (11–18 m)	**Deep dive:** Usually raises tail flukes
Group size: Up to 6	**Blow:** Distinctive: tall and V-shaped
Breaching: Frequent, various angles	

1:100

Gray Whale
Eschrichtius robustus

*One of the most familiar and popular whales
among whale watchers.*

IDENTIFICATION: The Gray Whale is similar in length to several of the other great whales. The body is stocky with a small, tapering head. When viewed from the side, the forehead is angled down steeply in front of the blowholes, giving the head shape a distinctly triangular appearance. The blow varies between bushy and column-shaped, attaining a height of up to five meters. In calm conditions the blow may appear V- or heart-shaped. The head is covered in small depressions, each containing whiskers. When the mouth is open, the creamy-white to yellow baleen plates contrast with the gray lips. The jawline is slightly arched. There is no dorsal fin; instead, a low hump is situated two-thirds of the way along the back, behind which a series of knuckles lead down toward the tail flukes. The tail flukes, which are up to 9.8 feet (3 m) from tip to tip, are triangular with a deep central notch and pointed tips. After a series of shallow dives, the tail flukes are generally thrown high into the air before a deep dive. The color of the skin is very distinctive, being predominantly gray but covered in white, yellow and orange patches. These pale patches, which are most striking around the head, are formed by encrusting barnacles, orange sealice and scars left by previous parasites. This gives the Gray Whale a mottled appearance, although young animals tend to be more uniformly gray.

SIMILAR SPECIES: The upright V-shaped or heart-shaped blow and the absence of a dorsal fin distinguish the Gray Whale from all the other large whales of the region, apart from the North Pacific Right Whale (page 76). However, Gray Whales lack the uniformly dark body coloration and distinctive pale callosities on the head, which are a feature of the North Pacific Right Whale. At long range, confusion with the Sperm Whale (page 96) is also possible, although this species differs in its offshore distribution, uniform coloration, wrinkled skin and angled blow.

BEHAVIOR: Gray Whales are one of the most energetic large whales, frequently engaging in spyhopping, lobtailing and breaching. They are also known to lie on their sides while waving one flipper in the air and spend a lot of time very close to shore, where they have developed a passion for surfing waves.

Uniquely among baleen whales, the Gray Whale is primarily a bottom-feeder. Dives may reach 394 feet (120 m), but feeding generally occurs in much shallower water. While feeding, the whale rolls onto its side and sucks sediment up into its mouth. Once the whale has gathered a mouthful of sediment, the silt and water are sieved out through the coarse baleen plates with the help of the tongue. In their summer feeding grounds, Gray Whales feed predominantly on small sea-floor crustaceans, but during migration they will also filter-feed on small fish and have even been documented off the coasts of California and Oregon skim feeding on krill.

Adult length: 39.4–45.9 ft (12–14 m)	**Deep dive:** Tail flukes raised
Group size: Up to 10, sometimes more	**Blow:** Tall and bushy
Breaching: Frequent, variable angles	

1:100

Mating and calving occurs in protected lagoons along the Pacific coast of Baja California during the winter. During this period, the whales are at their most social and mating activity is intense. Courtship often involves three or more animals. Other females, which conceived during the previous winter, are now ready to give birth. The calves remain in the safety of the lagoons for two or three months, building up their fat reserves for the northward migration. Mothers and calves travel very close to shore during migration, as this is the time they are most vulnerable to attack by transient Killer Whales.

STATUS AND DISTRIBUTION: The Gray Whale undertakes one of the longest annual migrations of any mammal. Each year they journey between their southern breeding lagoons in Baja California and their northern feeding grounds off Alaska, a round trip of 12,000 miles (19,000 km). During migration, whales can be seen from boats and headlands along the entire coast of the North American Pacific. The whales are present on their Arctic feeding grounds in the Bering, Chukchi and western Beaufort seas between April and November. As the ice begins to form in October they start to migrate south, reaching their Mexican breeding grounds between December and February. Whales are present on the breeding grounds, which extend as far as the Midriff Islands in the Gulf of California, until April. The return migration lasts from February to July. Every year, small numbers of animals spend the summer off the coasts of British Columbia, Washington, Oregon and northern California and do not complete the long migration.

Historically, Gray Whales inhabited the coastal waters of both the North Pacific and the North Atlantic. This made them easily accessible to early whalers. By the 18th century, the North Atlantic population was extinct. The Pacific population also appeared to be heading for extinction until the species was afforded legal protection in 1946. Since this time, Gray Whales in the North American Pacific have made a dramatic recovery. Today, they are probably close to their original pre-whaling population and are currently estimated to number around 23,000. In contrast, Gray Whales have not fared so well in the western North Pacific where only a few hundred are estimated to survive. This population still suffers from whaling exploitation and is considered to be highly endangered.

In the USA, Gray Whales were taken off the Endangered Species List in 1994, the first species of large whale to achieve that distinction. However, from 1999–2001 there was a large mortality along the west coast of North America. Several hundred whales were found dead during this period and calf production dropped significantly. Some scientists speculated that this may be due to the population reaching the number the ecosystem could sustain. However, other, more convincing evidence suggested that the mortality was the result of prolonged ice cover on their feeding grounds as a result of La Niña, a period of cooler-than-average ocean temperatures following a strong El Niño year.

Humpback Whale
Megaptera novaeangliae

One of the most acrobatic and best-known of the great whales.

IDENTIFICATION: The Humpback Whale is a large, stocky animal, black or dark gray in color, with a broad head covered in fleshy tubercles. One of the most distinctive features of this species is that it has extremely long, mostly white pectoral flippers. The dorsal fin is usually short and stubby and situated two-thirds of the way along the back toward the tail flukes. The blow is dense and mushroom-shaped. Before a deep dive, the body usually arches steeply before the tail flukes are raised high above the surface. The trailing edge of the flukes is always irregular and the unique patterning on the underside can be used to identify individuals.

SIMILAR SPECIES: At a distance, Humpback Whales could be confused with Sperm Whales (page 96) or any of the larger baleen whales. However, when seen well, the long flippers, fluke pattern and surfacing sequence separates the Humpback Whale from all other species.

BEHAVIOR: Humpback Whales are very demonstrative, regularly breaching, lobtailing and slapping pectoral flippers on the surface of the water. They can also be quite inquisitive and will occasionally approach whale watching boats or passing ships. Humpback Whales are very vocal animals and are known as the "singing whales." Although they normally travel singly or in very small pods, large congregations are not uncommon on the summer feeding grounds.

STATUS AND DISTRIBUTION: The Humpback Whale is found in all the world's oceans. It is a strongly migratory species, favoring cold, temperate waters in the summer and moving to warmer, tropical waters in the winter to mate and calve. In the North American Pacific, the summer feeding grounds include continental shelf waters from southern California north to the Gulf of Alaska. Large numbers summer in Alaskan waters, where important feeding areas include Glacier Bay, Frederick Sound and Prince William Sound. California also represents a major feeding ground, with notable concentrations occurring around the Farallon Islands off San Francisco, in Monterey Bay and around the Channel Islands off Santa Barbara. Alaskan Humpback Whales spend the winter months off Hawaii, while those animals summering between California and Washington winter along the coast of Baja California and mainland Mexico. The Humpback Whale was once believed to be one of the most abundant great whales in the North Pacific, with an estimated population of 15,000 prior to 1905. They were subsequently very heavily exploited by the whaling industry, and when afforded full protection in 1966 less than 1,000 animals remained. However, the species has made a good recovery and there may now be more than 6,000 throughout the entire North Pacific.

Adult length: 36–49 ft (11–15 m)	**Deep dive:** Usually raises tail flukes
Group size: Up to 10, sometimes more	**Blow:** Variable; tall, vertical and bushy
Breaching: Very frequent, variable angles	

1:100

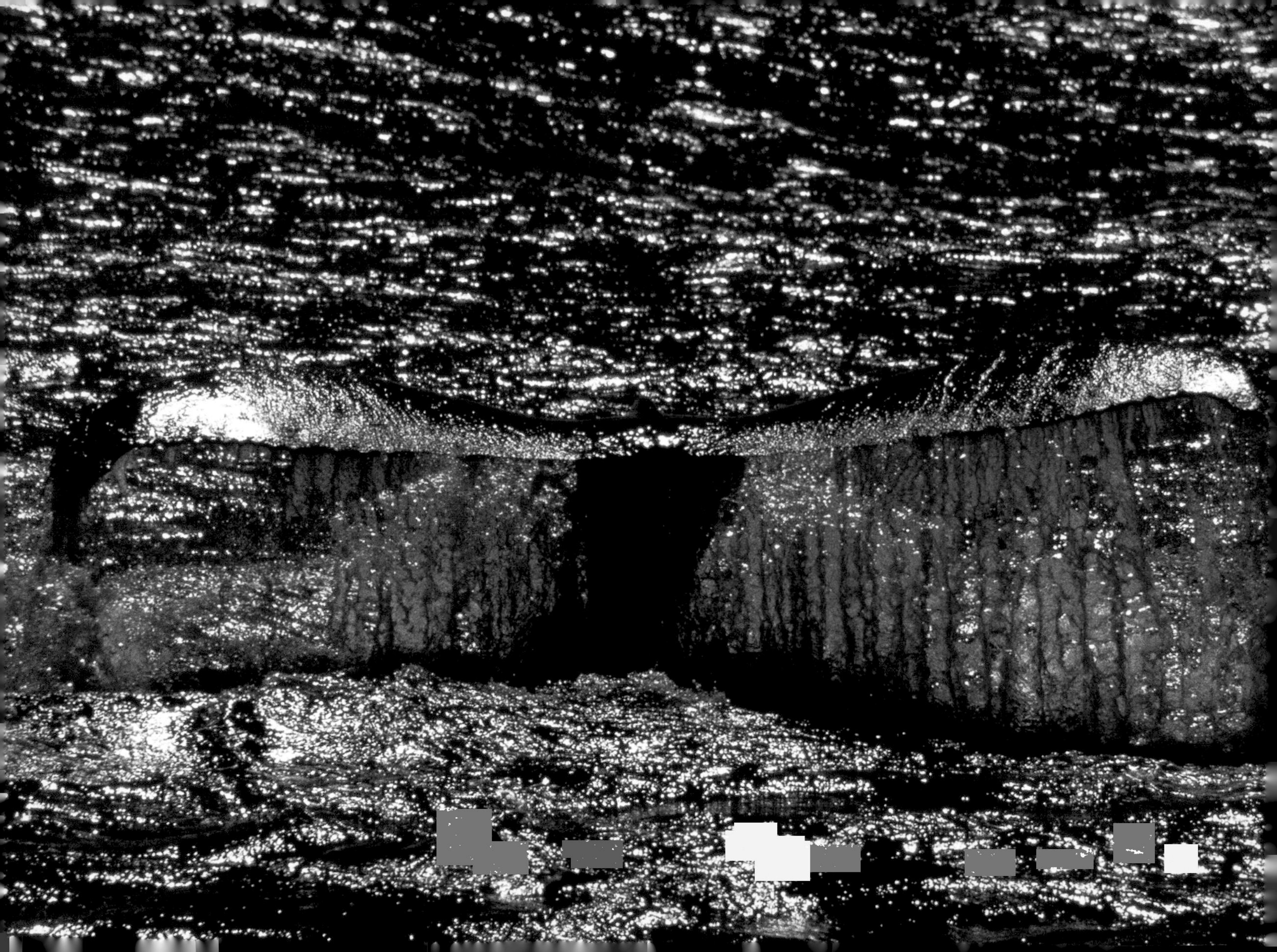

Blue Whale
Balaenoptera musculus

The largest animal ever to have lived on Earth.

IDENTIFICATION: The body of the Blue Whale is streamlined, with a broad, rounded head, prominent splashguard and a single ridge forward of the blowholes. The dorsal fin is very small relative to body size, situated far along the back toward the tail flukes and is usually only observed just before a deep dive. When surfacing, the Blue Whale raises its massive shoulders and splashguard farther out of the water compared with other rorquals. The tail flukes are crescent-shaped and appear slim compared to the very thick tail stock. The skin color is dark bluish-gray, distinctly mottled with light gray blotches. Blue Whales exhale a massive column-shaped blow which can reach a height of 39 feet (12 meters).

SIMILAR SPECIES: At long range Blue Whales can be confused with Fin Whales (page 88). Both species are very large; have a tall, vertical blow; and a uniform, grayish back. At relatively close range, Blue Whales are distinctly mottled and lack the pale chevrons often shown by Fin Whales. The Fin Whale also has a narrower, more pointed rostrum, a smaller splashguard, and a white right lower jaw. The Blue Whale has a relatively small fin which is often not seen until a deep dive, whereas the Fin Whale usually displays its prominent large fin on each surfacing. Unlike Fin Whales, Blue Whales may raise their tail flukes above the surface when making deep dives.

BEHAVIOR: Blue Whales are usually found singly or in pairs, although larger aggregations are found where there is a rich source of food. They are so massive that breaching is rare. Immature animals probably breach most regularly, and adults do not usually complete a full-body breach. They feed almost exclusively on krill and are occasionally observed lunge feeding at the surface.

STATUS AND DISTRIBUTION: Blue Whales are found in all the world's oceans and occur in continental shelf waters and in deep waters farther offshore. They favor cold temperate waters in the summer and are thought to migrate to tropical and warm temperate waters in the winter where breeding occurs. In the North American Pacific, the Blue Whale is distributed from Baja California to the Gulf of Alaska. They are typically first seen off Baja California in February, with numbers peaking in April. Good numbers are seen throughout Californian waters, particularly between July and November, where the population has recently been estimated at 2,200. This appears to be the largest population of the species anywhere in the world and notable hot spots include the Channel Islands, Monterey Bay and the Cordell Bank just north of San Francisco.

Adult length: 72.2–88.5 ft (22–27 m)
Group size: 1–2, sometimes more
Breaching: Only young known to breach, usually at a 45° angle
Deep dive: Sometimes raises tail flukes
Blow: An enormous vertical column

1:100

Fin Whale
Balaenoptera physalus

One of the fastest of the great whales, sometimes referred to as the greyhounds of the sea.

IDENTIFICATION: The Fin Whale is a very large species, second only in size to the Blue Whale. It is a relatively slender, streamlined species with a pointed head and a prominent dorsal fin positioned three-quarters of the way along the back. The fin is broad-based, swept back and often blunt at the tip. The upper side of the body is dark gray, often with pale chevrons behind the blowholes, while the underside is white. At close range, the pigmentation of the lower jaw is diagnostic, the left being dark and the right being white. The tall, column-shaped blow can reach a height of 33 feet (10 m).

SIMILAR SPECIES: At long range the Fin Whale is most likely to be confused with Sei (page 90), Bryde's (page 92) or Blue Whales (page 86). Compared with Sei and Bryde's Whales, the Fin Whale generally has a taller blow and the dorsal fin usually appears after the blow has dissipated. Also, on a deep dive the Fin Whale is more likely to arch its tail stock and the dorsal fin does not stand as upright as either of these species. Fin Whales differ from Blue Whales in having a relatively large dorsal fin that appears more rapidly after the blow on surfacing. Unlike Blue Whales, Fin Whales very rarely raise their tail flukes on diving. Caution should be exercised when trying to identify immature Fin Whales since they are easily confused with Bryde's and Sei Whales. Generally, the leading edge of the dorsal fin of the latter two species is much more erect than that of a Fin Whale.

BEHAVIOR: Fin Whales are usually observed singly or in pairs, sometimes in small pods, and occasionally in large aggregations where food is plentiful. They are very fast swimmers and have regularly been recorded lunge feeding and occasionally breaching.

STATUS AND DISTRIBUTION: The Fin Whale occurs throughout the world in both nearshore waters and deep waters beyond the edge of the continental shelf. In the North American Pacific, it occurs during the winter from central California south to the Sea of Cortez, although most of this population is believed to winter far offshore. In the summer they are regularly seen in pelagic waters from the Gulf of Alaska as far south as central Baja California. Numbers peak in early summer in southern Alaska and British Columbia, and there is an increase in abundance in the summer and fall off central California. Fin Whales occur year-round in the Gulf of California, with an increase in abundance during winter and spring. The population of Fin Whales in the North Pacific was heavily reduced by whaling, but since it has been fully protected numbers have increased to an estimated 14,000.

Adult length: 59–75 ft (18–23 m)	**Deep dive:** Tail flukes not raised
Group size: Up to 6, sometimes more	**Blow:** Very tall, vertical column
Breaching: Infrequent, variable angles	

1:100

Sei Whale
Balaenoptera borealis

One of the least well-known of the great whales.

IDENTIFICATION: The Sei Whale is similar in form and color to the Fin Whale (page 88), but is smaller with an erect, sickle-shaped dorsal fin situated two-thirds of the way along the back. When surfacing, the blowholes and dorsal fin appear simultaneously. While feeding, the back and dorsal fin are usually visible for a longer period compared with other rorquals. A single median ridge on the head extends from the blowhole to the tip of the rostrum. The skin color is dark gray on the upper back, flanks and lower jaw and often has distinct pale blotches. The belly is pale.

SIMILAR SPECIES: The Sei Whale is difficult to identify at sea, due to confusion with both Fin and Common Minke Whales (page 94). The most conclusive feature for separating the Sei Whale from the Fin Whale is the color of the lower lips. On the Sei Whale both lower lips are dark gray; on the Fin Whale the right lower lip is white and left is dark gray. At longer range a combination of features should be used to separate these species. Compared with the Fin Whale, the Sei Whale usually has a shorter blow which appears simultaneously with a higher, more erect dorsal fin. Unlike Fin Whales, Sei Whales rarely arch their tail stock prior to a deep dive. Sei Whales are distinguished from Common Minke Whales by their larger size and more prominent blow. In the southernmost part of their range, Sei Whales are very readily confused with Bryde's Whales (page 92). A close view of the head will reveal that the Sei Whale has a single ridge on the upper surface of the rostrum, whereas Bryde's Whales have three parallel ridges.

BEHAVIOR: Sei Whales tend to travel alone or in small groups. Unlike other rorquals, they often skim feed just below the surface. When feeding in this manner they can be quite unobtrusive, with only the occasional blow or top of the dorsal fin being visible. Sei Whales are very fast swimmers, but do not appear to be as demonstrative as either Fin or Common Minke Whales.

STATUS AND DISTRIBUTION: The Sei Whale has a cosmopolitan distribution, generally favoring temperate to subpolar waters and usually restricted to deep, pelagic waters. The Sei Whale appears to be widely but sparsely distributed in the North American Pacific from the Gulf of Alaska to central Mexico. There is a general northward shift of the population in the summer, with small numbers occurring in pelagic waters of the Gulf of Alaska south to central California. Recent surveys have shown that the species is rare in waters south of California, although there have been a handful of records from the Gulf of California. The Sei Whale was heavily exploited by whalers throughout its range and it is estimated that fewer than 10,000 animals now remain in the North Pacific.

Adult length: 39–53 ft (12–16 m)	**Deep dive:** Tail flukes not raised
Group size: Up to 6, sometimes more	**Blow:** Tall, thin and vertical
Breaching: Seldom observed	

1:100

Bryde's Whale
Balaenoptera edeni

Largely restricted to warm waters in the south of the region, this is one of the least well-known of the great whales.

IDENTIFICATION: Bryde's Whale is similar in shape and size to the Sei Whale (page 90). The rostrum is moderately pointed and has three prominent parallel ridges running along its upper surface between the tip and the blowholes. This feature is diagnostic if the head can be clearly viewed. The dorsal fin is large and upright in relation to the body and located about two-thirds of the way along the back toward the tail flukes; it is often irregularly notched or frayed on its rear margin. The upper side of the body is dark gray, sometimes irregularly covered in small, pale blotches. The sides and underside are paler gray. The surfacing sequence is characteristic, with the blowholes disappearing from view just before the fin appears. Bryde's Whale often surfaces at a steep angle, showing much of the head and rolling sharply before arching the back and tail stock. They do not usually raise their flukes prior to diving.

SIMILAR SPECIES: Bryde's Whale may be confused with several other rorquals, particular the Sei Whale from which it is probably impossible to separate unless seen at close range. The presence of head ridges is the only reliable feature for telling these two species apart, Bryde's having three ridges, whereas Sei has only one. Bryde's Whale can be distinguished from Fin Whale (page 88) by the smaller size, more pointed dorsal fin and dark right and left lower lips. Similarly sized immature Fin Whales can be extremely difficult to tell apart, although Bryde's Whales generally have a more erect dorsal fin and display more erratic surfacing movements. They can be separated from Common Minke Whales (page 94) by their larger size and taller, more conspicuous blow.

BEHAVIOR: Bryde's Whales are usually observed alone or in pairs. They can occasionally be inquisitive and will approach boats. When feeding they may swim erratically, frequently changing direction. This behavior is more reminiscent of a huge dolphin than a whale. The species sometimes breaches clear of the water.

STATUS AND DISTRIBUTION: Bryde's Whale is distributed throughout the world, primarily between latitudes 40°N and 40°S. It occurs both in coastal waters and deep pelagic waters. In the North American Pacific, Bryde's Whales are distributed widely throughout tropical and warm temperate waters, occurring north of Baja California only rarely. It is the most common baleen whale in the Gulf of California, where it is found throughout the year. The status and abundance of Bryde's Whale in the North American Pacific is unknown. However, unlike other large baleen whales, this species was not heavily targeted by whalers and most commercial whaling was limited to the western Pacific. It is believed still to be relatively abundant throughout the tropical and subtropical Pacific.

Adult length: 36–49 ft (11–15 m)	**Deep dive:** Tail flukes not raised
Group size: Up to 3, occasionally more	**Blow:** Tall, thin and vertical
Breaching: Occasional, variable angles	

1:100

Common Minke Whale
Balaenoptera acutorostrata

The smallest baleen whale to be found in the North American Pacific.

IDENTIFICATION: The Common Minke Whale has a slender and streamlined body, with a sharply pointed rostrum which is bisected by a single longitudinal ridge beginning in front of the blowholes. The upper parts are dark gray, lightening to white on the belly and the underside of the flippers. The dorsal fin is prominent and sickle-shaped, and located two-thirds of the way along the back toward the tail flukes. The blow is inconspicuous and vertical, the blowhole appearing almost simultaneously with the dorsal fin. A distinctive feature, although only visible at close range, is a diagonal white band on the upper surface of the flippers. Like the Fin Whale (page 88), it often arches its tail stock prior to a deep dive, and does not normally raise its tail flukes clear of the surface.

SIMILAR SPECIES: The Common Minke Whale is most likely to be confused with the larger rorquals, particularly Bryde's (page 92), Sei (page 90) and Fin Whales, which are extremely similar in shape. However, the much smaller size, white flipper bands and lack of a tall blow should distinguish it from these species. If seen poorly, Common Minke Whales may be confused with beaked whales, which appear similar at the surface. However, the pointed rostrum with a central ridge of Common Minke Whale is diagnostic. In addition, Common Minke Whales generally have a larger, more sharply sickle-shaped dorsal fin than the beaked whales.

BEHAVIOR: Common Minke Whales are usually solitary, sometimes seen in pairs or small groups and rarely in larger aggregations. They can be very elusive and difficult to follow when feeding actively, but are sometimes quite inquisitive, occasionally spyhopping or approaching passing boats. Breaching is regularly observed, particularly during periods of rough weather. Like Fin Whales, Common Minke Whales are capable of short bursts of high speed. During fast travel they create a large "rooster tail" splash, not unlike that of a Dall's Porpoise (page156), which is easily observed at a distance.

STATUS AND DISTRIBUTION: Common Minke Whales occur throughout the northern hemisphere, but are generally more common in cooler waters than in the tropics. They favor nearshore waters over the continental shelf and frequently enter bays and estuaries, though are sometimes encountered in offshore pelagic waters. The species is found throughout the North American Pacific, but is not considered to be abundant except in Alaskan waters. In the extreme north of their range, Common Minke Whales are believed to be migratory, but do occur throughout the year off Washington and California. During the winter, small numbers are seen from at least northern Washington south to the equator.

Adult length: 23–33 ft (7–10 m)	**Deep dive:** Tail flukes not raised
Group size: Up to 4	**Blow:** Small, vertical and bushy, but usually not visible
Breaching: Occasional, variable angles	

1:100

Sperm Whale
Physeter macrocephalus

One of the most accomplished divers, able to reach depths of over 3,200 feet (1,000 m) and to remain submerged for over 90 minutes.

IDENTIFICATION: Sperm Whales are the largest of the toothed whales, with mature males being much larger than females. The body is robust, with a massive blunt head that comprises almost one-third of the animal's total length. The lower jaw is long, narrow and inconspicuous. Sperm Whales appear slate-gray or brown and the skin is usually wrinkled. A single nostril is located on the left side of the front of the head, resulting in a distinctive bushy blow that is angled forward. There is no dorsal fin, only a small hump, behind which is a series of knuckles running as far as the tail flukes. The flukes, which are generally raised vertically prior to a deep dive, are large and triangular with smooth edges and a deep central notch.

SIMILAR SPECIES: The Sperm Whale overlaps in size with several baleen whales and, like the Humpback (page 82), North Pacific Right (page 76), Blue (page 86) and Gray Whales (page 78), it raises its flukes before a deep dive. However, the Sperm Whale lacks the twin blowhole and vertical blow characteristic of all baleen whales; the blowhole is also situated much closer to the front of the head. The other species that, like the Sperm Whale, lack a distinctive dorsal fin are the Gray Whale and the North Pacific Right Whale (which has no fin at all). However, these two species show pale patches around the head, whereas the skin of the Sperm Whale is uniformly dark and usually wrinkled.

BEHAVIOR: Sperm Whales are gregarious and often occur in pods of up to 20 or more, although mature males are often solitary on summer feeding grounds. They can be quite demonstrative and breach regularly. This species is renowned for diving to tremendous depths and regularly remains submerged for over an hour. These energy-sapping dives are often followed by lengthy recuperation periods when the whale lies motionless at the surface, blowing regularly.

STATUS AND DISTRIBUTION: The Sperm Whale is widely distributed in deep, offshore waters throughout the world. Mixed pods of females and immature males usually remain in tropical to warm temperate waters throughout the year. In spring, groups of males travel to higher latitudes. Sperm Whales are found throughout the North Pacific during the summer, with most of the population moving southwards to below 40°N during the winter months. In the North American Pacific, groups are often found along seamounts and deep sea canyons. The species is present throughout the year in Californian waters, and is particularly abundant in spring and fall, although remaining far from shore. Farther north in Washington and Oregon, they are only seen in the spring, summer and fall. Sperm Whales are also abundant in tropical waters south of the USA.

Adult length: 36–59 ft (11–18 m)
Group size: Up to 20, sometimes more
Breaching: Frequent, variable angles
Deep dive: Usually raises tail flukes
Blow: Moderately tall and bushy, angled forward

1:100

Pygmy Sperm Whale
Kogia breviceps

A diminutive whale that is unobtrusive and rarely seen.

IDENTIFICATION: The Pygmy Sperm Whale is very small and porpoise-like in shape, having a short, robust body with a rounded head and no beak. It has a small narrow jaw that is situated beneath a large squared-off forehead. The blowhole is offset slightly to the left of the center of the head. The dorsal fin is positioned just behind the midpoint of the back and is broad-based, narrowing to a pointed tip, which is usually swept backwards. A series of indistinct notches run along the spine between the dorsal fin and the tail flukes. The upper parts are gray, fading to paler gray on the flanks and white or pink on the belly. A light-colored, bracket-shaped mark behind the eye gives the impression of a gill cover, resulting in the Pygmy Sperm Whale having a superficially shark-like appearance.

SIMILAR SPECIES: The distinctive body shape and lethargic behavior of the Pygmy Sperm Whale help to distinguish it from similarly-sized dolphin species. At a distance, this whale may also be mistaken for some of the smaller beaked whales, although Pygmy Sperm Whales are much smaller and lack a protruding beak. The Pygmy Sperm Whale differs from the slightly smaller, but very similar, Dwarf Sperm Whale (page 100) by its smaller, sickle-shaped dorsal fin, which is positioned farther than halfway along the back.

BEHAVIOR: Due to the small number of live sightings, little is known about the behavior of Pygmy Sperm Whales at sea. This whale is typically seen only in the calmest sea conditions, when it is generally observed moving slowly or hanging motionless at the surface with only the head and upper body showing. On diving, the body tends to sink below the surface, without rolling forward or raising its tail flukes. The species has generally been observed alone or in small groups of between two and six individuals, and appears to be shy of boats. Vertical breaches have been recorded. When disturbed, animals sometimes emit a reddish-brown anal liquid.

STATUS AND DISTRIBUTION: Most information on the distribution of Pygmy Sperm Whales comes from stranded animals. It occurs throughout the world in deep temperate to tropical waters but is considered to be rare throughout its range. The very limited number of sightings may be due to a combination of its shy behavior and its ability to remain submerged for lengthy periods. Stranding records from the North American Pacific indicate that the Pygmy Sperm Whale is widely distributed in small numbers from Washington south to Baja California. It seems likely that it favors offshore regions beyond the edge of the continental shelf.

Adult length: 8.9–12 ft (2.7–3.7 m)	**Deep dive:** Tail flukes not raised
Group size: Up to 6	**Blow:** Short and faint
Breaching: Occasional, leaps vertically	

1:33

Dwarf Sperm Whale
Kogia sima

The world's smallest whale, which is rarely seen and little known.

IDENTIFICATION: The Dwarf Sperm Whale is almost identical to the Pygmy Sperm Whale (page 98) in form and color. It is dolphin-sized with a robust body and a relatively tall, centrally positioned dorsal fin. The dorsal fin is broad at the base, usually rising to a blunt tip (although it can be pointed), behind which there may be a series of small ridges running along the spine toward the tail. The short, rounded head lacks a beak. Instead, set below and beneath the forehead are the narrow jaws. The blowhole is positioned slightly to the left of the top of the head and the blow is low and inconspicuous. The pointed flippers are positioned well forward on the body. There are no striking markings on the upper side, which is a fairly uniform dark gray, fading to white or pink on the belly. White patches are sometimes apparent around the head. A conspicuous pale bracket-shaped line runs behind the eye on both sides of the face. This marking, and the underslung jaw, give the Dwarf Sperm Whale a rather shark-like appearance, which may act as a deterrent to predators.

SIMILAR SPECIES: The Dwarf Sperm Whale is superficially similar in size and shape to several species of dolphin and porpoise, but the blunt forehead lacking a beak, and generally lethargic behavior are distinctive. Separation from the very similar Pygmy Sperm Whale is much more challenging. The Dwarf Sperm Whale is slightly smaller in size, with a much larger, less sickle-shaped dorsal fin positioned centrally on the back. Dwarf Sperm Whales lack the pronounced concave area around the blowhole of the Pygmy Sperm Whale.

BEHAVIOR: Most encounters with Dwarf Sperm Whale involve animals traveling slowly or resting at the surface. Surfacing movements are lethargic and unobtrusive, although breaching has been recorded occasionally. Dives generally involve the animal sinking out of sight without rolling forward or raising its tail flukes. The species is generally shy, but when basking at the surface sometimes tolerates a close approach. When disturbed, Dwarf Sperm Whales may emit a reddish-black jet of "ink" as a defense mechanism. At sea, group sizes tend to number less than ten individuals.

STATUS AND DISTRIBUTION: The Dwarf Sperm Whale is globally distributed in warm temperate to tropical seas. It appears to favor deep waters beyond the edge of the continental shelf. While the distribution of this species remains something of a mystery due to its inconspicuous nature, it is regularly sighted in the Gulf of California, which is one of the best places in the world to see this elusive whale.

Adult length: 6.9–9.2 ft (2.1–2.8 m)	**Deep dive:** Tail flukes not raised
Group size: Up to 10	**Blow:** Short and faint
Breaching: Occasional, leaps vertically	

1:50

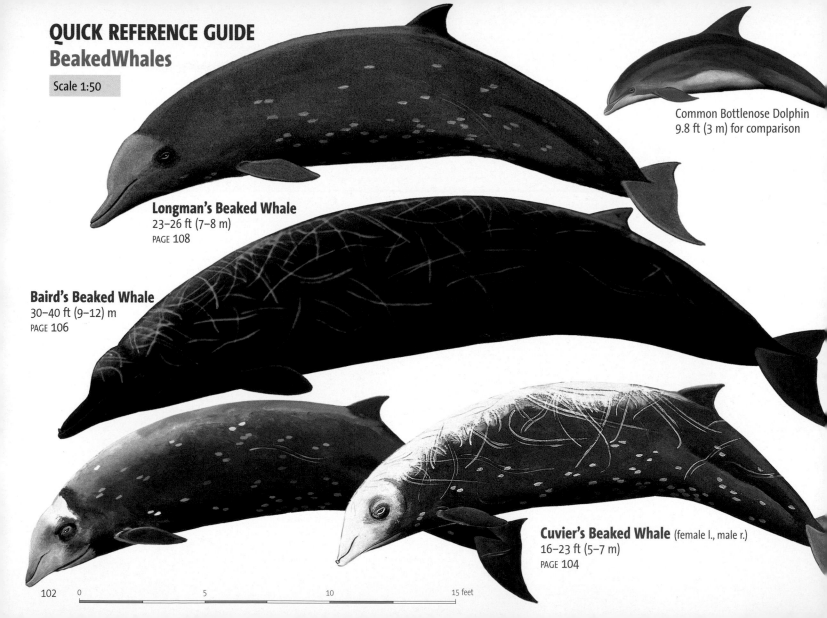

QUICK REFERENCE GUIDE
BeakedWhales

Scale 1:50

Common Bottlenose Dolphin
9.8 ft (3 m) for comparison

Longman's Beaked Whale
23–26 ft (7–8 m)
PAGE 108

Baird's Beaked Whale
30–40 ft (9–12) m
PAGE 106

Cuvier's Beaked Whale (female l., male r.)
16–23 ft (5–7 m)
PAGE 104

0   5   10   15 feet

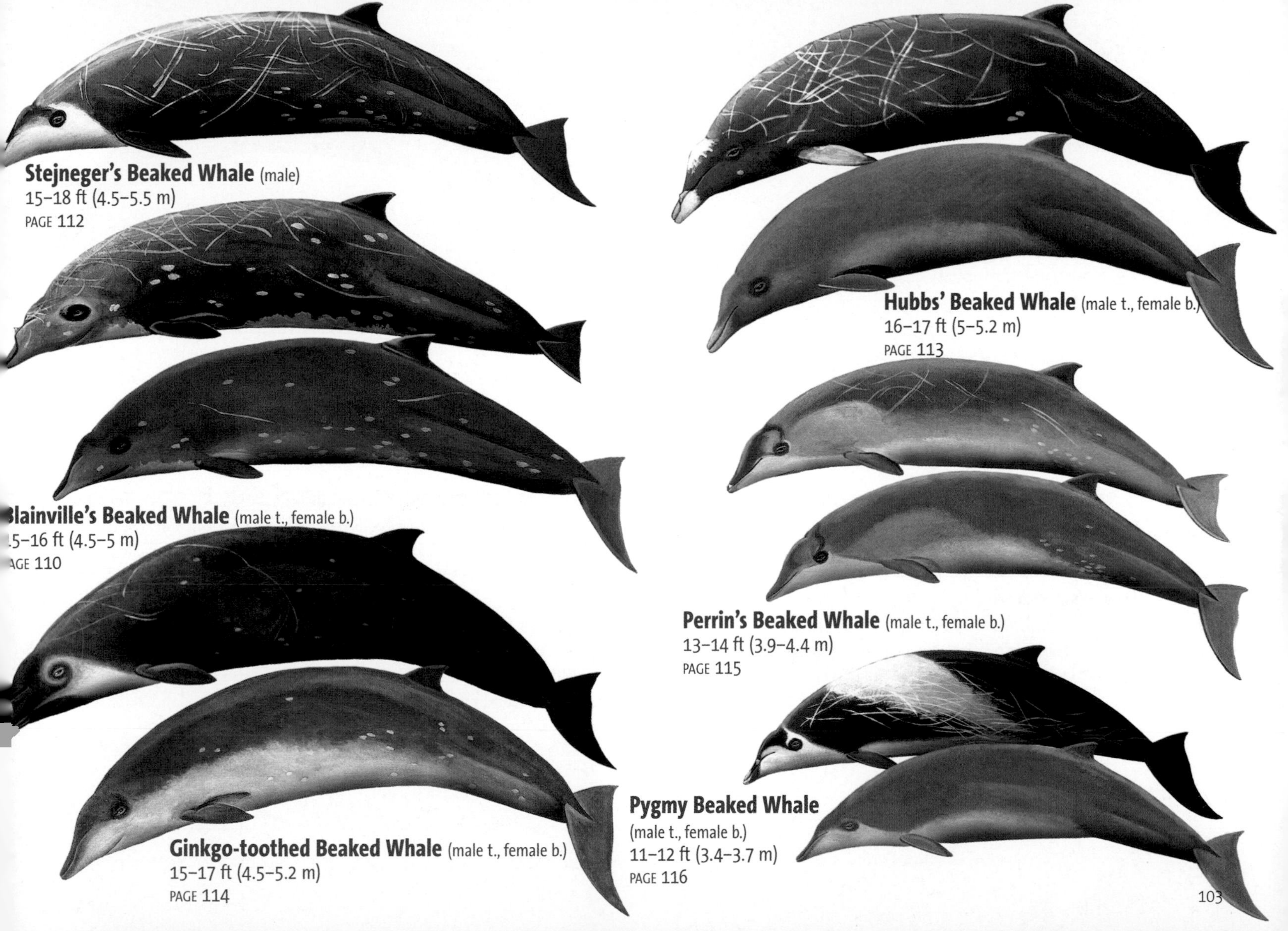

Stejneger's Beaked Whale (male)
15–18 ft (4.5–5.5 m)
PAGE 112

Hubbs' Beaked Whale (male t., female b.)
16–17 ft (5–5.2 m)
PAGE 113

Blainville's Beaked Whale (male t., female b.)
15–16 ft (4.5–5 m)
PAGE 110

Perrin's Beaked Whale (male t., female b.)
13–14 ft (3.9–4.4 m)
PAGE 115

Ginkgo-toothed Beaked Whale (male t., female b.)
15–17 ft (4.5–5.2 m)
PAGE 114

Pygmy Beaked Whale
(male t., female b.)
11–12 ft (3.4–3.7 m)
PAGE 116

Cuvier's Beaked Whale
Ziphius cavirostris

The most widespread and best-known of the world's beaked whales.

IDENTIFICATION: Cuvier's Beaked Whale is a medium-sized whale and one of the largest and most robust of the beaked whales, with a small sickle-shaped dorsal fin and grayish to orange-brown coloration. It is best identified by its size, coloration and head-shape. The forehead slopes gently to a relatively short beak, which has a peculiar, curved mandible, resembling the beak of a goose. Two conical teeth erupt on adult males at the tip of the lower jaw. Mature adults sometimes develop completely pale heads, and, in some cases, pale coloration may extend along the back as far as the dorsal fin. The upper body is sometimes heavily scarred, indicating that the individual is an adult male that has been involved in fighting. The blow is barely visible, up to 3.3 feet (1 m) tall, and directed slightly forward. The flukes are unnotched and rarely lifted clear of the surface prior to a deep dive.

SIMILAR SPECIES: Cuvier's Beaked Whale may be confused with all other beaked whales in the North American Pacific. It can be distinguished from Baird's Beaked Whale (page 106) and Longman's Beaked Whale (page 108) by its smaller size, shorter beak and lack of a steep forehead, and from beaked whales of the genus *Mesoplodon* by its distinctive head shape, peculiar beak and larger, more markedly falcate dorsal fin. Without a clear view of the head, reliable identification is extremely difficult.

BEHAVIOR: Given the limited number of sightings at sea, the behavior of Cuvier's Beaked Whale is still poorly known. Particularly pale, scarred animals have been observed alone, or among tight pods of 3 to 10 darker animals. It is possible that these scarred individuals are sexually mature males that have been involved in fights while competing for females. Solitary mother and calf pairings have sometimes been observed away from larger pods. Although they often avoid vessels, pods have sometimes been seen moving leisurely alongside passing ships. Breaching is occasionally observed.

STATUS AND DISTRIBUTION: Cuvier's Beaked Whale is found throughout the world's oceans, ranging from cold temperate waters to tropical seas. Like other members of the beaked whale family, they are found almost exclusively in deep, pelagic waters and are often associated with canyons and escarpments on the edge of the continental shelf. In the North American Pacific, the limited number of sightings and strandings would indicate that this species is distributed continuously from Alaska to the equator. Although considered to be the most common beaked whale along the west coast of North America, sightings are still relatively uncommon, and mostly from pelagic waters off California and Baja California.

Adult length: 16–23 ft (5–7 m) **Group size:** Up to 12 **Breaching:** Occasional, leaps almost vertically	**Blow:** Short and bushy, angled slightly forward

1:50

Baird's Beaked Whale
Berardius bairdii

The largest and most frequently observed beaked whale in the region.

IDENTIFICATION: Baird's Beaked Whale has a long, rotund body and a proportionately small, triangular dorsal fin situated more than two-thirds of the way along the back toward the tail flukes. The forehead slopes quite steeply to a long, cylindrical beak. Both sexes have a pair of triangular teeth that erupt near the tip of the lower jaw. The skin color is generally slate-gray to brown. However, the upper parts of both males and females are often heavily scarred, which can result in the animal appearing pale overall. This species is often found in large groups and can therefore be detected at long distances, which is unusual for any beaked whale. The blow is short, bushy, and very dense.

SIMILAR SPECIES: Head shape separates Baird's Beaked Whale from Cuvier's Beaked Whale (page 104) and the similar-sized Common Minke Whale (page 94). In addition, Common Minke Whales have a more markedly falcate dorsal fin and usually show white bands on their pectoral flippers. Longman's Beaked Whale (page 108) is very similar in shape and size to Baird's Beaked Whale, but has a proportionately larger, more erect dorsal fin and a steeper forehead. Although similar in appearance, Baird's Beaked Whale is significantly larger than all of the *Mesoplodon* beaked whales, having a relatively small dorsal fin in relation to its body length than species in this genus.

BEHAVIOR: Baird's Beaked Whale is highly gregarious, with close-knit pods of up to 30 animals regularly being encountered, often surfacing and submerging in unison. Although generally boat-shy they very occasionally tolerate a close approach. When traveling, they roll sharply at the surface, sometimes lifting their tail flukes clear of the water before a deep dive. Although usually undemonstrative, acrobatic behavior including breaching and lobtailing is observed more frequently than in most other beaked whales.

STATUS AND DISTRIBUTION: Baird's Beaked Whale is endemic to the deep offshore waters of the North Pacific. In the North American Pacific the species has been sighted in virtually all areas from southern Alaska to northern Baja California, usually in pelagic waters beyond the 3,300-foot (1,000-m) depth contour. It is seen with some regularity off central California north to the eastern Gulf of Alaska, and appears to be migratory, occurring closer to shelf waters during summer and fall. Records are less frequent during the colder winter months, when it is presumed the animals move farther offshore. This species is occasionally encountered during pelagic whale watching trips off Baja California, California and Washington.

Adult length: 30–40 ft (9–12 m)	**Deep dive:** Sometimes raises tail flukes
Group size: Up to 30, sometimes more	**Blow:** Short and bushy, angled slightly forward
Breaching: Occasional, variable	

1:50

Longman's Beaked Whale
Indopacetus pacificus

One of the most recently described beaked whales, which has a predominantly tropical distribution.

IDENTIFICATION: Longman's Beaked Whale is a large beaked whale. It has a long, cylindrical body, short, tapered flippers, and broad, unnotched flukes. The beak is prominent and relatively long. The dorsal fin is tall with a long base, usually sickle-shaped and located two-thirds of the way along the body toward the tail flukes. This species has the largest dorsal fin of all the beaked whales. It usually has a large melon, which in some individuals rises perpendicularly from the beak. Adults have a distinct "crease" between the melon and the beak. Although there has been no confirmed sighting of an adult male, it seems likely that, as in other beaked whales, they have protruding teeth situated at the tip of the lower jaw. The coloration of adults has been variously described as gray to light brown, although some animals have linear scars. Young animals are quite distinctly patterned, being dark gray-brown with a conspicuous pale melon and white sides.

SIMILAR SPECIES: Longman's Beaked Whale could be confused with Baird's Beaked Whale (page 106), Cuvier's Beaked Whale (page 104) or several of the *Mesoplodon* beaked whales. However, it has a shorter and less robust beak than Baird's Beaked Whale and a larger, more pronounced melon and dorsal fin; it should also be readily separated from all other beaked whales in the North American Pacific by its larger size, bulbous head and prominent dorsal fin.

BEHAVIOR: Like many species of beaked whale, basic aspects of the natural history of Longman's Beaked Whale remain unknown. From the few reliable sightings at sea it would appear to be a gregarious species with a mean pod size of about 20 animals. When traveling at the surface they can be rapid swimmers, often raising the beak and melon up out of the water as they move in a close-knit group. They have been observed in association with dolphins on several occasions.

STATUS AND DISTRIBUTION: The majority of sightings of Longman's Beaked Whale have been confined to tropical and subtropical pelagic waters of the Pacific and Indian oceans. Sightings have been made in all months of the year, indicating that this species is resident in the tropics. Although it has occurred occasionally off Baja California, all such sightings have occurred during El Niño events when warmer-than-normal sea surface temperatures were recorded. There was a single sighting in pelagic waters off Oregon in 2003; this represents the most northerly record of the species. Given the small number of sightings and the low number of strandings, this is considered to be a relatively rare species throughout its range.

Adult length: 23–26 ft (7–8 m)	**Breaching:** Occasional
Group size: Up to 30	**Blow:** Short and bushy

1:50

Blainville's Beaked Whale
Mesoplodon densirostris

The world's best-known species of **Mesoplodon** *beaked whale.*

IDENTIFICATION: Blainville's Beaked Whale is a small, slim whale with a spindle-shaped body and a thick, moderately long beak. It has a small dorsal fin that is triangular to falcate in shape and located beyond the midpoint of the back. The flippers are short and tapered and the flukes unnotched. Mature animals can be identified readily at sea by the unique shape of the head and beak. The forehead is flattened in front of the blowhole and the lower jaw is distinctly arched, a feature that is more noticeable in females and immatures of this species than in any other *Mesoplodon* beaked whale. The dramatic curve of the jawline is usually clearly visible above the water when the whale surfaces, generally lifting its beak out of the water at a 45° angle. Adult males have two large, almost conical teeth protruding from the apex of the arch of the lower jaw, which are visible above the animal's head. Adults are dark overall, though the color can vary from brown to dark bluish-gray, and adult males, in particular, often show heavy scarring. The lower flanks and ventral surfaces are lighter and are usually quite pale in immature animals.

SIMILAR SPECIES: Blainville's Beaked Whale is likely to be confused only with other beaked whales. Given good views, the characteristic contour of the mouth and the two large, compressed teeth should separate mature males from all other species. Females and immature animals are extremely difficult to identify at sea unless they are accompanied by an adult male.

BEHAVIOR: Compared with other *Mesoplodon* beaked whales, the behavior of Blainville's Beaked Whale is relatively well-known. Much of the information on this species has originated from studies of small populations in the Bahamas and Hawaii. They are regularly recorded in small groups of up to seven animals which generally consist of adult females and juveniles but are sometimes accompanied by a single mature male. It is possible that sexually mature males move between pods of adult females as a mating strategy. This species can be quite demonstrative and has been observed breaching almost vertically clear of the surface.

STATUS AND DISTRIBUTION: This is the most widely distributed *Mesoplodon* beaked whale and occurs in tropical and warm temperate waters throughout the world's oceans. It is regularly found in pelagic waters between 656 and 2,300 feet (200–700 m) deep, often close to offshore islands. In the North Pacific this species is regularly seen around Hawaii and strandings are frequent along the coast of southern Japan. However, it would appear to be scarce in the North American Pacific, with just a couple of strandings from California and a few recent sightings from the Gulf of California and the coastal waters of central Mexico.

Adult length: 15–16 feet (4.5–5 m)	**Breaching:** Occasional
Group size: Up to 7	**Blow:** Inconspicuous and bushy

1:50

Stejneger's Beaked Whale
Mesoplodon stejnegeri

The most northerly beaked whale in the region, though very rarely seen.

IDENTIFICATION: The Stejneger's Beaked Whale is very similar in structure to other *Mesoplodon* beaked whales. It has a spindle-shaped body, smoothly sloping forehead, a relatively long, well-defined beak and a prominent, falcate dorsal fin situated two-thirds of the way along the back toward the tail flukes. Adult males have two large teeth, each of which protrudes from the forward edge of a raised area on the side of the lower jaw. The jawline of females and subadult males is much straighter. Few animals have been seen at sea, but their coloration has been described as dark gray or grayish-brown on the upperside with paler underparts. Adults usually have pale blotches on the flanks and undersides, with adult males having long scratches over much of the body. Adult females have been recorded showing variable white markings on the undersides of their tail flukes.

SIMILAR SPECIES: Stejneger's Beaked Whale is most likely to be confused with Hubbs' Beaked Whale (page 113). However, the very prominent white "cap" on the head of mature male Hubbs' Beaked Whales appears to be diagnostic. Confusion is possible with Blainville's Beaked Whale (page 110), although this species has a more pronounced arched jawline and tends to occur in more southerly latitudes. It may also be confused with Pygmy Beaked Whale (page 116) and Perrin's Beaked Whale (page 115), although these two species are smaller and the males have smaller, less protruding teeth. Stejneger's Beaked Whale could also be confused with Cuvier's Beaked Whale (page 104), but the short beak and distinct coloration of the latter species should be diagnostic. It also overlaps in range with Baird's Beaked Whale (page 106), though this species is considerably larger and has a pronounced melon.

BEHAVIOR: With only a handful of live sightings, the behavior of Stejneger's Beaked Whale remains largely unknown. It usually occurs in pods of two to six, although groups of up to 15 individuals have been recorded. Groups typically comprise individuals of varying size, age and sex, and animals have been observed swimming abreast in close-knit pods surfacing and submerging in unison.

STATUS AND DISTRIBUTION: Much of what is known about the distribution of Stejneger's Beaked Whale has been inferred from stranding records and a small number of sightings at sea. These records suggest that it is restricted to the subarctic and cold temperate waters of the North Pacific. In the North American Pacific it appears to range from the Bering Sea south to central California. As with other members of the beaked whale family, sightings have been restricted to deep, pelagic waters beyond the edge of the continental shelf.

Adult length: 15–18 ft (4.5–5.5 m)		**Breaching:** Unknown
Group size: Up to 15		**Blow:** Unknown

1:50

Hubbs' Beaked Whale
Mesoplodon carlhubbsi

One of the least known of all the beaked whales and very rarely seen at sea.

IDENTIFICATION: Adult male Hubbs' Beaked Whales have a distinctive raised white cap, just in front of the blowhole. The forehead slopes quite steeply to a prominent, robust beak, which is also usually white in mature males. The jawline is strongly arched, with two protruding compressed teeth. In females and subadult males, the beak is longer and slimmer, the teeth are not exposed, and the jawline forms a distinct S-shaped curve. The falcate dorsal fin is situated two-thirds of the way along the back toward the tail flukes. The skin color has been described as uniformly black to dark-gray, although females and subadults are usually paler. Adult males are heavily scarred, while scarring on females and subadult males is less pronounced. The blow is low and inconspicuous.

SIMILAR SPECIES: The most common beaked whale that overlaps in range with Hubbs' Beaked Whale is the Cuvier's Beaked Whale (page 104). Males of the latter species lack the arched jawline, and the pair of protruding teeth are positioned at the tip of the lower jaw. There are at least five other species of *Mesoplodon* beaked whale in the North American Pacific that could easily be confused with Hubbs' Beaked Whale: Stejneger's Beaked Whale (page 112), Ginkgo-toothed Beaked Whale (page 114), Blainville's Beaked Whale (page 110), Perrin's Beaked Whale (page 115) and Pygmy Beaked Whale (page 116). Given a close view, an adult male Hubbs' Beaked Whale should be readily distinguished from males of these species by a combination of its raised white cap, strongly arched jawline, and robust, partially white beak. It

is virtually impossible to separate females and subadult males from other *Mesoplodon* beaked whales at sea. If seen at long range, the overall dark coloration and position of the dorsal fin could lead to confusion with the Common Minke Whale (page 94). However, at closer range the differences in head and body shape, and the characteristic beak should distinguish Hubbs' Beaked Whale from this species.

BEHAVIOR: With very few sightings at sea, the behavior of Hubbs' Beaked Whale is poorly known. They travel in pods of 10 or less, appear to be shy, and do not approach ships. The extent of scarring seen on several individuals suggests that there is considerable aggression between adult males.

STATUS AND DISTRIBUTION: Information on the distribution of Hubbs' Beaked Whale is based primarily on a few stranding records and sightings at sea. It appears to be confined to the cold temperate waters of the eastern and western North Pacific. In the North American Pacific it has been found stranded from southern California to British Columbia. Like other *Mesoplodon* beaked whales, Hubbs' Beaked Whale is probably largely restricted to deep pelagic waters.

Adult length: 16–17 ft (5–5.2 m)	**Breaching:** Unknown
Group size: Unknown	**Blow:** Low and inconspicuous

1:50

Ginkgo-toothed Beaked Whale
Mesoplodon ginkgodens

One of the least-known of all whales and very rarely seen at sea.

IDENTIFICATION: Like other *Mesoplodon* beaked whales, the Ginkgo-toothed Beaked Whale has a slender, spindle-shaped body with a relatively small head. The forehead slopes smoothly to a prominent beak. The lower jaw is arched and, in adult males, a single tooth erupts from the apex of the raised area, approximately halfway along the jawline on each side of the head. These two flattened teeth resemble the leaf of a ginkgo tree, although only the tips of these teeth erupt above the gums. The dorsal fin is located about two-thirds of the way along the back from the head, is falcate to triangular in shape and may have a hooked tip. The body coloration has been described as black or dark gray, becoming pale on the underside. Males appear to be less heavily scarred compared with other *Mesoplodon* beaked whales. Females are likely to be similar in color to males and have paler heads and underparts.

SIMILAR SPECIES: Ginkgo-toothed Beaked Whale is very difficult to identify at sea and is likely to be confused with all the other beaked whale species occurring in the region. Only adult male animals are likely to be identifiable with any certainty. The most likely confusion species, based on size and overlapping ranges, are Hubbs' Beaked Whale (page 113) and Blainville's Beaked Whale (page 110). The Ginkgo-toothed Beaked Whale lacks the raised white forehead of Hubbs' Beaked Whale and the flattened forehead, pronounced arched jaw and larger teeth of Blainville's Beaked Whale. Its range may overlap with Pygmy Beaked Whale (page 116) and Perrin's Beaked Whale (page 115), but Ginkgo-toothed Beaked Whale should be distinguishable from both these species by its larger size and distinctive head shape. Female and immature animals are extremely difficult to identify unless accompanied by an adult male. Longman's Beaked Whale (page 108) may overlap in range, but is larger and has a bulbous melon and well-defined beak. Confusion is possible with Cuvier's Beaked Whale (page 104), but this species is larger and has a shorter beak with, in males, the exposed teeth positioned at the tip.

BEHAVIOR: With so few sightings, very little is known about the behavior of the Ginkgo-toothed Beaked Whale. It is likely to be unobtrusive and the lack of scarring may indicate that males are less aggressive compared to other beaked whale species.

STATUS AND DISTRIBUTION: The small number of strandings indicates that the Ginkgo-toothed Beaked Whale is distributed in warm temperate and tropical waters of the North Pacific and Indian Oceans. The majority of strandings has occurred in the western North Pacific. In the North American Pacific, there have been a couple of strandings in southern California and on the west coast of Baja California.

Adult length: 15–17 ft (4.5–5.2 m)	**Breaching:** Unknown
Group size: Unknown	**Blow:** Unknown

1:50

Perrin's Beaked Whale
Mesoplodon perrini

The most recently discovered species of whale in the world, only being described in 2002. It is known from just five specimens that washed ashore along the California coast between 1975 and 1997 and is named as a tribute to the eminent American cetacean biologist Dr. William Perrin.

IDENTIFICATION: Perrin's Beaked Whale is one of the smallest *Mesoplodon* beaked whales, with a spindle-shaped body, broad tail stock and short, unnotched tail. The melon forms a small bulge and the jawline is straight. In adult males a pair of protruding teeth is present at the apex of the lower jaw. The dorsal fin is small and triangular, and situated two-thirds of the way along the back toward the tail flukes. Adult males are dark gray on the upper parts, grading to white on the underparts, and have a dark gray marking extending from the corner of the mouth and encompassing the eye and the rostrum. They may also bear a number of white linear scars on their upper flanks, probably inflicted by the teeth of other males of the species.

SIMILAR SPECIES: The small size of the Perrin's Beaked Whale should distinguish it from all other beaked whales in the North Pacific with the exception of Pygmy Beaked Whale (page 116). However, good views would be necessary to separate even adult males of these two species. Given a close view the forward position of the teeth on male Perrin's Beaked Whale and its straighter jawline should distinguish it from the Pygmy Beaked Whale. Females and immature animals would be very difficult to separate from the latter species unless accompanied by an adult male.

BEHAVIOR: There have been no confirmed sightings of Perrin's Beaked Whale at sea and therefore nothing is known of their behavior.

STATUS AND DISTRIBUTION: Perrin's Beaked Whale was described almost 30 years after the discovery of the first specimen. This followed a re-examination of the remains of the stranded whales using new DNA analytical techniques. This proved that the specimens were in fact a species new to science. The stranding pattern of the five animals is suggestive of an eastern North Pacific distribution, but this number of records is too small to be able to draw any firm conclusions about the status and distribution of the species.

Adult length: 13–14 ft (3.9–4.4 m)		**Breaching:** Unknown	
Group size: Unknown		**Blow:** Unknown	

1:50

Pygmy Beaked Whale
Mesoplodon peruvianus

The world's smallest species of beaked whale, only officially described in 1991.

IDENTIFICATION: The Pygmy Beaked Whale, like other *Mesoplodon* beaked whales, has a slender, spindle-shaped body, short, tapered flippers and un-notched tail flukes. The tail stock and tail flukes are relatively broad and robust, the head is quite small and narrow, and the beak is relatively short. There have been no confirmed live sightings of adult males, but from examination of stranded specimens it seems likely that adult males have two protruding teeth situated well behind the tip of the beak on the lower jaw. The females lack protruding teeth. The dorsal fin is small, triangular-shaped and situated two-thirds of the way along the back toward the tail flukes. The body is uniformly dark gray lightening to pale gray on the underside. Some individuals show a broad pale area across the shoulders and upper flanks that forms a conspicuous chevron when viewed from above. This species appears generally to show little body scarring, but some animals, presumably males, have many scratches over the shoulders, flanks and lower half of the tail stock.

SIMILAR SPECIES: The Pygmy Beaked Whale is only likely to be confused with other *Mesoplodon* beaked whales. However, its very small size, relatively broad and robust tail stock and tail flukes, and distribution should help to separate it from other beaked whales that occur in the North American Pacific.

BEHAVIOR: Due to the very recent discovery of the Pygmy Beaked Whale, and the scarcity of sightings, very little is known about its behavior. Most of the sightings have consisted of small groups or pairs, although strandings have usually been of solitary animals.

DISTRIBUTION: The Pygmy Beaked Whale appears to be distributed primarily in deep, pelagic waters of the eastern tropical Pacific, particularly off Peru, although it has also been recorded in New Zealand. In the North American Pacific there have been at least two strandings off Bahía la Paz in Baja California. There have been a few sightings recorded during recent pelagic cetacean surveys off central Mexico and Guatemala.

Adult length: 11–12 ft (3.4–3.7 m)	**Breaching:** Unknown
Group size: Up to 3	**Blow:** Unknown

1:50

Mesoplodon Beaked whale identification

Nine species of beaked whale are known to occur in the North American Pacific. All of them are challenging to identify at sea, although Baird's Beaked Whale, Longman's Beaked Whale and Cuvier's Beaked Whale are distinctive given good views. By far the most difficult cetaceans to identify in the North American Pacific are the *Mesoplodon* beaked whales, of which six species are known to occur. The sighting of a *Mesoplodon* beaked whale at sea is generally considered to be an exceptional event due to the shy habits, unobtrusive behavior and apparent "rarity" of all species throughout their known range in deep, offshore waters. Unfortunately, because *Mesoplodon* beaked whales are so difficult to identify at sea, most sightings are not recorded to species. There are still only a handful of photographs taken at sea, and most are of stranded animals, which reveal little about their true coloration or their surfacing behavior. The illustration opposite is an artist's impression of the diagnostic features that are required to confirm identification of each species based on current knowledge. A close view of the head of an adult male is crucial to the positive identification of all *Mesoplodon* beaked whales in the North American Pacific. It is important to note that, although the plate shows the whales raising their heads clear of the water, it is not known whether all of the species regularly do this when surfacing (although some have been seen to do so).

Blainville's Beaked Whale
Forehead slopes gently to a moderately long beak. Arched lower jaw with erupting teeth.

Hubbs' Beaked Whale
Distinctive raised white cap. Steep forehead, prominent beak. Strongly arched lower jaw with two erupting teeth at the apex of the arch.

Pygmy Beaked Whale
Small size, pale area across shoulder. Arched lower jaw with probably two teeth on lower jaw well back from the tip of the beak.

Stejneger's Beaked Whale
Forehead slopes smoothly to relatively large beak. Arched lower jaw with pair of large protruding teeth at the forward edge of the raised arch.

Perrin's Beaked Whale
Small size, pair of protruding teeth on lower jaw just back from the tip of the beak.

Ginkgo-toothed Beaked Whale
Arched lower jaw with protruding teeth at the forward edge of the raised arch.

Scale 1:50

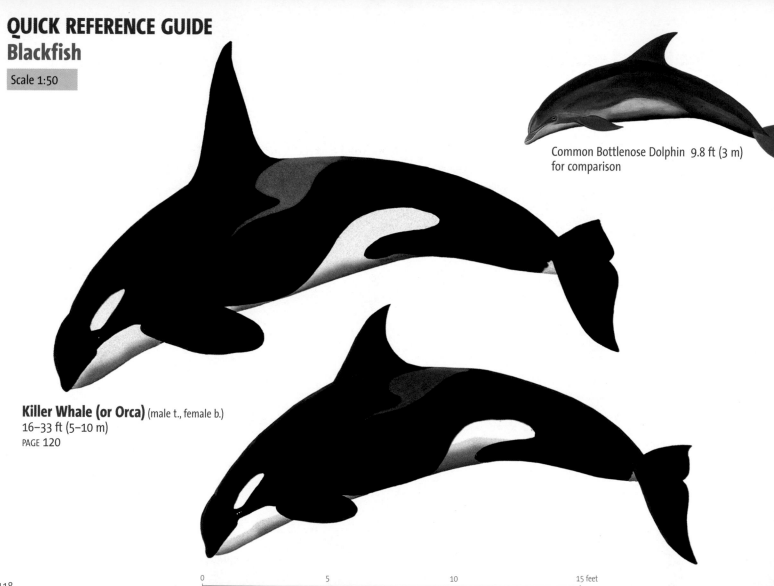

Common Bottlenose Dolphin 9.8 ft (3 m)
for comparison

Killer Whale (or Orca) (male t., female b.)
16–33 ft (5–10 m)
PAGE 120

0   5   10   15 feet

False Killer Whale
13–20 ft (4–6 m)
PAGE 126

Pygmy Killer Whale
6.5–8.9 ft (2–2.7 m)
PAGE 128

Short-finned Pilot Whale (male t., female b.)
12–21 ft (3.5–6.5 m)
PAGE 124

Melon-headed Whale
6.5–8.5 ft (2–2.6 m)
PAGE 130

Killer Whale (or Orca)
Orcinus orca

A supremely powerful marine predator that occurs throughout the region.

IDENTIFICATION: Despite its name, the Killer Whale is in fact the largest of the dolphins, and perhaps the most striking and familiar of all cetaceans. The stocky, sleek black-and-white body and prominent dorsal fin are unmistakable. The oval head tapers to an indistinct beak and the rounded jaws are lined with sharp teeth. The shape and size of the dorsal fin varies depending on the age and sex of the individual, adult males being the most distinctive, with a broad, triangular dorsal fin reaching up to 6.5 feet (2 m) in height. Female and immature animals are significantly shorter in body length, with smaller, sickle-shaped dorsal fins. Killer Whales spend their lives in discrete family groups so most sightings involve individuals with different shaped dorsal fins. Unusually for a dolphin, the flippers are broad and paddle-shaped. The blow is tall, vertical and bushy. The black and white coloration of the Killer Whale is diagnostic. The majority of the upper side of the animal is black but there is a striking white patch positioned just behind the eye. This gives the species a fierce, large-eyed appearance. Most animals show a gray saddle behind the dorsal fin which is highly variable in shape and extent. The underside of the tail flukes is white with a dark border and the white on the throat extends along the chest and belly, widening to form a patch on the lower flanks.

SIMILAR SPECIES: In poor light, or at long range, when the white eye patch is not visible, it is possible to mistake female or subadult Killer Whales for other members of the blackfish family or large dolphins with tall dorsal fins, such as the Risso's Dolphin (page 134). In combination, the tall dorsal fin, white eye patch and gray saddle are features unique to Killer Whales.

BEHAVIOR: The Killer Whale generally travels in family pods of between 2 and 15 animals. Lone individuals are rarely sighted but pods sometimes join together to form single units of over 100 animals. Killer Whales are often very active at the surface, where they are frequently observed breaching, spyhopping, lobtailing and flipper slapping. They also engage in other surface activities including beach rubbing, logging and dorsal fin slapping. Despite their inquisitive nature, Killer Whales rarely bow ride or wake ride passing vessels.

Adult length: 16–33 ft (5–10 m)	**Breaching:** Frequent, variable angles
Group size: Family groups of 2–30	**Blow:** Moderately tall and bushy

1:100

The Killer Whale is an extremely powerful marine hunter. At up to 10 tons (9 metric tonnes) in weight and 33 feet (10 m) in length, with a swimming speed of over 28 mph (44 km/h), it is capable of hunting fish, seabirds, marine mammals and even great white sharks. Known as the "wolves of the sea," Killer Whales hunt in highly coordinated family groups and in this way are able to subdue prey species larger than themselves, even including the largest baleen whales. Despite their fearful name and appetite for just about everything on the à la carte seafood menu, a deliberate attack by a Killer Whale on a human being has yet to be recorded in the wild.

STATUS AND DISTRIBUTION: The Killer Whale is the most widespread marine mammal in the world, occurring in all oceans from the tropics to the edge of the pack ice in both the northern and southern hemispheres. This species generally becomes more abundant at higher latitudes, but its distribution is always patchy and may change with shifting food abundance. In the North American Pacific, there are several regions where Killer Whales are present throughout the year, with recognizable pods forming part of ongoing long-term research programs. In other regions, Killer Whales may pass through on their way from one hunting ground to another, or appear seasonally to hunt a specific prey species. The unpredictable nature of Killer Whales makes them even more exciting to watch, especially as they can appear anywhere and at any time.

Killer Whales are present along the entire coast of the North American Pacific, although in coastal waters they are most abundant where prey species such as seals, sea lions and salmon gather in large numbers. Although many pods appear to have distinct and relatively local home ranges, others move over vast areas.

Photo identification work has revealed that some individuals range from Alaska to as far as California.

Research work based on genetics, acoustics and movements has identified three different forms of Killer Whale in the North American Pacific: these forms are referred to as resident, transient and offshore.

- Resident Killer Whales are generally coastal, fish-eating and, as their name suggests, stay faithful to a relatively local area. In British Columbia and Alaska, their movements tend to be associated with the nearshore migrations of salmon, which is their favored prey for at least half of the year.

- Transient Killer Whales roam over much larger areas in search of quite different prey. They are marine mammal hunters, feeding on many species of seals and cetaceans. In British Columbia, transients feed predominantly on Harbor Seals, and are often present in small groups of three to five individuals near seal haulout sites. Steller Sea Lions, California Sea Lions, Harbor Porpoises, Dall's Porpoises and Pacific White-sided Dolphins also form part of the staple diet. In California, larger prey are more frequently taken, particularly Gray Whales during the annual migration but even Blue Whales are sometimes attacked.

- Offshore Killer Whales probably roam over large areas of open ocean and are not currently known to mix with either residents or transients. These animals are poorly understood but they appear to be more closely related to residents than transients, being fish-eaters.

Short-finned Pilot Whale
Globicephala macrorhynchus

A common deep-water species, mainly recorded in the south of the region.

IDENTIFICATION: The Short-finned Pilot Whale is one of the most distinctive of all the cetaceans. The initial impression is that of a large, robust black dolphin with a bulbous head and a dorsal fin that is broad-based, sharply curved, round-tipped, and situated well forward on the back. Short-finned Pilot Whales generally travel in family groups, within which the age and sex of an individual can be determined by body size and the size and shape of the dorsal fin. The mature males are the most striking, being large with very broad, almost flag-shaped dorsal fins. Females and subadult males are smaller, with broad-based, falcate dorsal fins. Calves have dolphin-like, falcate dorsal fins. The head is thick and bulbous and the blow is short and bushy. The skin color is predominantly black, with a pale gray saddle behind the dorsal fin and a pale anchor-shaped patch below the throat. Before a deep dive the tail stock is lifted high and, occasionally, the tail flukes are raised clear of the water.

SIMILAR SPECIES: The bulbous head and distinctive dorsal fin distinguishes the Short-finned Pilot Whale from the much smaller Pygmy Killer Whale (page 128) and Melon-headed Whale (page 130). These features, combined with the pale saddle, also help to distinguish it from the similarly sized False Killer Whale (page 126). Short-finned Pilot Whales are easily told from Killer Whales by the absence of a white eye patch and the lack of a tall dorsal fin. They can also look similar to Risso's Dolphins (page 134) due to their size and bulbous foreheads, but lack the pale coloration and extensive scarring shown by this species.

BEHAVIOR: Short-finned Pilot Whales are usually seen in family groups traveling slowly at the surface or logging, often allowing a close approach by boats. Spyhopping, flipper slapping and lobtailing are regularly observed, although breaching and bow riding are rare. Having sighted a pod of Short-finned Pilot Whales, it is generally worth scanning nearby areas of sea as small subgroups may be spread out over a few kilometers. Each subgroup may be segregated, containing only adult males, females with young, or subadults. Sometimes groups travel in a chorus line and they frequently associate with other marine mammals.

STATUS AND DISTRIBUTION: The Short-finned Pilot Whale is commonly distributed in the tropical and subtropical oceans of the world. Although they may occur in nearshore waters, they are generally considered to be nomadic in deep offshore waters. In the North American Pacific, Short-finned Pilot Whales are abundant as far north as the border between the US and Mexico. In warm-water years, animals may venture as far north as the southern Gulf of Alaska.

Adult length: 12–21 ft (3.5–6.5 m)	**Breaching:** Occasional, usually at a low angle
Group size: Family groups of 2–50	**Blow:** Short and bushy

1:50

False Killer Whale
Pseudorca crassidens

A relatively little-known species, recorded occasionally in the south of the region.

IDENTIFICATION: The False Killer Whale is a very large member of the dolphin family. The body is long and slender and the head is small. The shape of the head, which is often lifted clear of the water when the animal is porpoising, is distinctively conical, tapering gently to a rounded jaw, which lacks a beak. The slender, dolphin-like dorsal fin may be blunt or pointed at the tip, and is positioned slightly behind the midpoint of the back toward the tail flukes. The long and pointed flippers, with an elbow halfway along the leading edge, are diagnostic and this feature may be seen when animals are bow riding. The skin color is almost entirely black, although there is a gray anchor-shaped patch below the throat, similar to that of the Short-finned Pilot Whale (page 124). There is also a light gray patch on the belly and some individuals show pale areas on the side of the head.

SIMILAR SPECIES: The False Killer Whale is similar in shape to the Melon-headed Whale (page 130) and Pygmy Killer Whale (page 128) but is much larger and more powerful in appearance. Confusion is perhaps most likely with female Killer Whales (page 120) or Short-finned Pilot Whales, although with good views the all-dark body distinguishes the False Killer Whale from the former, and the slender head and body, with a dolphin-like dorsal fin, from the latter. The position of the dorsal fin also differs from that of the Short-finned Pilot Whale, being set farther back along the body, close to the midpoint of the back.

BEHAVIOR: False Killer Whales are typically seen in family groups moving rapidly along the surface, with their heads and upper bodies raised clear of the water. They are very curious and will often approach boats in order to bow ride. At other times they travel at a more leisurely pace, often forming a chorus line formation. Although often found in association with other cetaceans, such as Common Bottlenose Dolphins (page 136) and Rough-toothed Dolphins (page 138), in the eastern tropical Pacific, False Killer Whales have been implicated in attacks on dolphins being released from tuna purse-seine nets. Pod sizes of several hundred are not uncommon, although groups of 10 to 20 are most frequent. This species is particularly prone to mass strandings.

STATUS AND DISTRIBUTION: Although widely distributed throughout the tropical and warm temperate oceans of the world, the False Killer Whale seems to be fairly uncommon throughout its range. In the North American Pacific, this species has a widespread distribution south of 30°N in offshore waters. It is rarely sighted north of southern California, although there have been records as far north as Alaska.

Adult length: 13–20 ft (4–6 m)	**Breaching:** Frequent, various angles
Group size: Family groups of 2–20, occasionally up to 200	**Blow:** Short and bushy

1:50

Pygmy Killer Whale
Feresa attenuata

A little-known species, only occasionally recorded in the region.

IDENTIFICATION: Pygmy Killer Whales are difficult to identify at sea, as the key features are subtle and not easily seen. They are fast-moving, dolphin-sized cetaceans with a relatively bulky body forward of the centrally positioned, falcate dorsal fin, the rear of the animal tapering to a thin tail stock. Identification is easiest when the Pygmy Killer Whale is bow riding. This allows the observer to look down on the animal and note its two most distinctive features: the shape of the head and the flippers. Pygmy Killer Whales have a rounded melon and lack a beak, and have long flippers that are broadly rounded at the tip. The color of the skin is dark gray, and there is a dorsal cape that is widest below the dorsal fin. The flanks are paler, and there are several areas that are often pale or white, including the lips, an anchor-shaped throat patch and the hindbelly.

SIMILAR SPECIES: The Pygmy Killer Whale is easily told from most dolphin species by the lack of a protruding beak. It could be mistaken for the much larger Short-finned Pilot Whale (page 124) or False Killer Whale (page 126). However, the Short-finned Pilot Whale differs in having a dorsal fin positioned forward of center on the back and a more bulbous melon, and the False Killer Whale has a more slender, tapering head shape. At distance, confusion is also possible with Risso's Dolphin (page 134), which on closer inspection is a uniquely pale dolphin with extensive scarring. Separation from the very similar Melon-headed Whale (page 130) is particularly difficult, but Pygmy Killer Whale has a more rounded melon, blunt tips to the flippers and often shows more extensive areas of white, particularly on the chin and toward the rear of the flank. The dorsal fin is also generally larger and more erect than that of the Melon-headed Whale.

BEHAVIOR: Pygmy Killer Whales tend to live in smaller pods than the more gregarious Melon-headed Whale, generally occurring in groups of 50 or less, although larger pod sizes of up to a few hundred have been known. Surface behavior can include spy-hopping, tail slapping and high leaps, though generally this species is not particularly acrobatic. When porpoising, animals often raise their heads clear of the water as they move rapidly forward in a chorus line.

STATUS AND DISTRIBUTION: The Pygmy Killer Whale is found throughout the tropical and, less frequently, subtropical to temperate oceans of the world. However, nowhere is it common and very little is known about its abundance or distribution. In the North American Pacific the species occurs as far north as the southern tip of Baja California, preferring the equatorial latitudes of the eastern tropical Pacific.

Adult length: 6.5–8.9 ft (2.0–2.7 m)	**Breaching:** Occasional
Group size: Generally up to 50	**Blow:** Generally not visible

1:33

Melon-headed Whale
Peponocephala electra

A little-known species, rarely recorded in the region.

IDENTIFICATION: The Melon-headed Whale is a small, sleek and dynamic cetacean. The overall shape of the body is slim, particularly the tail stock, which is long and narrow. The flippers are long and sharply pointed, and the dorsal fin is tall and falcate, being positioned centrally on the back. The head is relatively pointed (melon-shaped), but this feature can be difficult to observe at sea. The skin color is generally dark gray to black, with a variable dark cape that widens below the dorsal fin. In good light, the sides of the head also appear darker than the flanks, giving the animal a masked appearance. The lips, anchor-shaped throat patch and areas around the genitals are pale.

SIMILAR SPECIES: With the exception of the Pygmy Killer Whale (page 128), the Melon-headed Whale is quite unlike any of the similarly sized dolphins in shape and color. In poor light, or at a distance, the Melon-headed Whale can be confused with the Risso's Dolphin (page 134), but, given good views, confusion is most likely with other blackfish. Young False Killer Whales (page 126) and Short-finned Pilot Whales (page 124) both look similar, although the size of adults in both of these species is far larger than adult Melon-headed Whales. Pods comprising entirely immature Short-finned Pilot Whales or False Killer Whales are occasionally encountered, which could be misidentified as Melon-headed Whales. However, the Melon-headed Whale differs from the former species in having a centrally positioned dorsal fin and a less bulbous head, and from the latter due to its head shape, which is less triangular. The Melon-headed Whale is extremely similar to the Pygmy Killer Whale in size, shape and color, and is best told by the slightly pointed head shape, long pointed flippers and its smaller, less erect dorsal fin.

BEHAVIOR: The Melon-headed Whale is highly gregarious, with pod sizes ranging from 50 to 1,500. These large, tightly packed groups often move at high speed, porpoising out of the water at a shallow angle. Melon-headed Whales rarely form chorus lines, while Pygmy Killer Whales often do. They occasionally bow ride but are often wary and shy of vessels. In the eastern tropical Pacific, the species regularly associates with Fraser's Dolphins (page 146) and Rough-toothed Dolphins (page 138).

STATUS AND DISTRIBUTION: The Melon-headed Whale is distributed throughout the tropical and warm temperate waters of the world but is most frequently sighted in equatorial seas. It occurs at relatively low densities in offshore waters but little is known about its abundance or seasonal movements. Melon-headed Whales are very rare in the North American Pacific, being recorded only a few times in the Gulf of California.

Adult length: 6.5–8.5 ft (2–2.6 m)	**Breaching:** Occasional
Group size: Generally 50+	**Blow:** Inconspicuous, short and bushy

1:33

QUICK REFERENCE GUIDE
Dolphins and Porpoises

Scale 1:25

Common Bottlenose Dolphin
6.2–12.8 ft (1.9–3.9 m)
PAGE 136

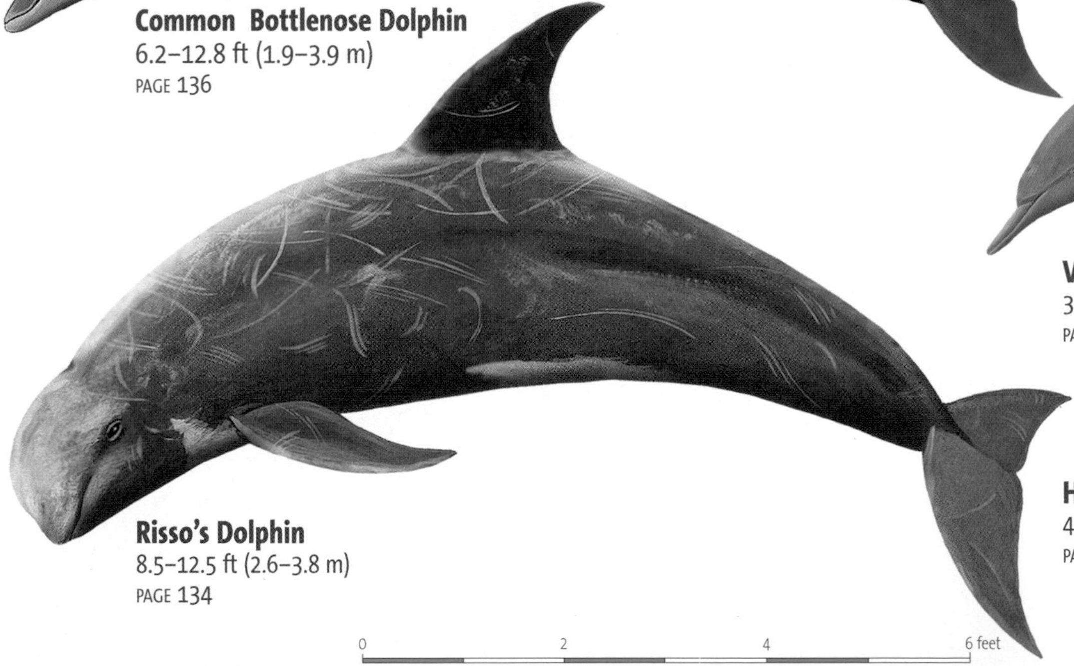

Risso's Dolphin
8.5–12.5 ft (2.6–3.8 m)
PAGE 134

Rough-toothed Dolphin
6.8–8.5 ft (2.1–2.6 m)
PAGE 138

Spinner Dolphin
5–7.2 ft (1.5–2.2 m)
PAGE 140

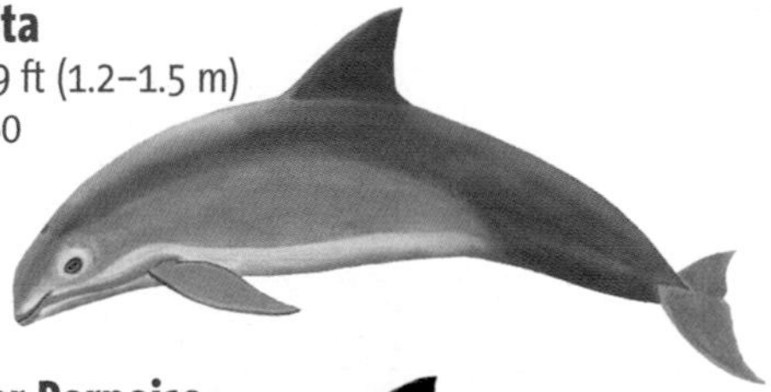

Vaquita
3.9–4.9 ft (1.2–1.5 m)
PAGE 160

Harbor Porpoise
4.9–5.9 ft (1.5–1.8 m)
PAGE 158

0   2   4   6 feet

Pacific White-sided Dolphin
5.6–8.2 ft (1.7–2.5 m)
PAGE 152

er's Dolphin
.5 ft (2–2.6 m)
146

t-beaked Common
hin
.2 ft (1.7–2.5 m)
148

-beaked Common
hin
.2 ft (1.7–2.5 m)
50

's Porpoise
.2 ft (1.7–2.2 m)
56

Striped Dolphin
5.9–8.5 ft (1.8–2.6 m)
PAGE 144

Pantropical Spotted
Dolphin
5.6–8.5 ft (1.7–2.6 m)
PAGE 142

Northern Right Whale Dolphin
6.6–10 ft (2–3.1 m)
PAGE 154

133

Risso's Dolphin
Grampus griseus

One of the most distinctive dolphins of the region.

IDENTIFICATION: The distinctive shape and coloration of the Risso's Dolphin means that it is unlikely to be confused with any other species at close range. Initial impressions are of a large, robust dolphin with a tall, falcate dorsal fin. It has a bulbous head with a short, indistinct beak, uniform dark gray to white coloration, and extensive criss-cross scarring all over the body. When they are born, calves are pale gray or brown with a cream belly, but darken to almost black as they mature. On reaching adulthood they become paler and more heavily scarred, though the dorsal fin and adjacent back often remain distinctly darker and the belly remains light gray to white, leading to an anchor-shaped patch on the chest.

SIMILAR SPECIES: The species most likely to be confused with Risso's Dolphin is the Cuvier's Beaked Whale (page 104), which can also appear extensively cream-colored and scarred on the upper surface. However, Risso's Dolphins are much smaller than Cuvier's Beaked Whales, in which the dorsal fin is positioned two-thirds of the way along the back toward the tail flukes, and which has a short but distinct beak. Risso's Dolphins are also similar in shape to several members of the blackfish family, particularly Short-finned Pilot Whales (page 124), with which they often associate. However, Risso's Dolphin differs from the Short-finned Pilot Whale in its smaller size and centrally positioned, falcate dorsal fin.

BEHAVIOR: The Risso's Dolphin feeds predominantly at night and spends much of the day engaged in slow travel or logging at the surface. Highly inquisitive animals, they often engage in breaching, spyhopping and tail slapping, but rarely bow ride. They are commonly seen in pods of 10 to 40 individuals and, on occasion, hundreds or even thousands of animals may gather together. Risso's Dolphin frequently associates with other cetaceans, particularly Pacific White-sided (page 152) and Northern Right Whale Dolphins (page 154), and Short-finned Pilot Whales.

STATUS AND DISTRIBUTION: Risso's Dolphin has a worldwide distribution in tropical to warm temperate waters. In the North American Pacific, it is regularly sighted over continental shelf and deep offshore waters from Washington in the north to the Gulf of California and the eastern tropical Pacific in the south. Off the US, the species tends to favor the warmer waters of California during the winter months, shifting northward into Oregon and Washington during spring and early summer. Farther south, the status of Risso's Dolphin is less well-known.

Adult length: 8.5–12.5 ft (2.6–3.8 m)	Group size: Up to 500, sometimes more

1:33

Common Bottlenose Dolphin
Tursiops truncatus

Perhaps the most familiar and well-known of all dolphins.

IDENTIFICATION: The Common Bottlenose Dolphin is a large, robust dolphin with a short, stubby beak that is clearly demarcated from the melon. The dorsal fin is centrally positioned along the back and is tall and falcate, being relatively thick and blunt at the tip. The flippers are moderately long and slender. The body is uniformly gray above, fading to paler gray on the flanks and paler still or pinkish on the belly. In some populations, a distinct cape is visible, but most Common Bottlenose Dolphins are plain gray on the upper side. The flippers and tail flukes are dark.

SIMILAR SPECIES: The large size, plain gray coloration and lack of distinct flank markings distinguish this species from most other dolphins. Confusion is possible with two uniformly colored small cetaceans; the Rough-toothed Dolphin (page 138) and the Harbor Porpoise (page 158). The distinct bulging forehead and short, stubby beak are diagnostic in separating it from the former, and the tall falcate dorsal fin from the latter.

BEHAVIOR: Common Bottlenose Dolphins are most commonly seen in pods of 2 to 15 individuals, but may occasionally form larger pods of several hundred. They are highly active and curious animals capable of traveling at great speed, and regularly ride in the bow wave or wake of passing ships; they are also capable of amazing acrobatics. Offshore, Common Bottlenose Dolphins are highly social and often occur in mixed pods with Short-finned Pilot Whales (page 124) or Risso's Dolphins (page 134). Pod sizes tend to be smaller in nearshore areas than in offshore pelagic zones.

STATUS AND DISTRIBUTION: A cosmopolitan species occurring throughout temperate and tropical seas of the world. In all oceans, Common Bottlenose Dolphins appear to be segregated into nearshore and offshore forms that are genetically distinct. In the North American Pacific, individuals from the offshore form are smaller and darker than those of the nearshore form. The nearshore form is found in coastal waters, including lagoons, estuaries, bays and harbors. This is the only dolphin that occurs regularly so close to shore and it is not unusual to see animals playing in the breaking surf. Populations of the nearshore form are often resident, but seasonal movements and home ranges vary between areas. In contrast, the offshore form appears to range over large areas of the pelagic temperate and tropical Pacific. In the North American Pacific, both the nearshore and offshore forms of the Common Bottlenose Dolphin show little seasonal shift in distribution, being widespread as far north as California, although they may occur farther north during warm-water years.

| **Adult length:** 6.2–12.8 ft (1.9–3.9 m) | **Group size:** Up to 50, sometimes more |

1:33

limit of nearshore form

Rough-toothed Dolphin
Steno bredanensis

One of the least well-known of the dolphins in the region and perhaps the most reptilian in appearance.

IDENTIFICATION: The Rough-toothed Dolphin is a medium-sized, relatively robust dolphin and has a distinctive conical head shape with a low melon and a long, slender beak. Unlike other long-beaked dolphins, there is no differentiation between the beak and the forehead, giving it a slightly reptilian appearance. The dorsal fin is wide at the base and erect and pointed. The flippers are larger and set farther back on the body than other dolphins of a similar size. Mature males may also have a bulge on the underside of the tail stock. The upper back is dark gray, forming a distinctive cape. This becomes lighter toward the flanks, which often have white or pinkish blotches. The belly and underside of the tail stock are usually white. The beak may also show whitish or pinkish patches, particularly around the lips, and, in some populations, these markings extend to form a white throat. The coloration and patterning of adults may vary considerably, but immatures generally have less distinct patterning.

SIMILAR SPECIES: The Rough-toothed Dolphin is similar to the Common Bottlenose Dolphin (page 136) in size and in having a dark gray body. However, when seen well, the distinctive head shape, with no crease between the melon and beak should distinguish the Rough-toothed Dolphin from all other dolphin species.

BEHAVIOR: The Rough-toothed Dolphin is a relatively poorly known species which has been seen most frequently in groups of between 10 and 20 animals, although pods of over 100 have been reported. It is not a particularly active dolphin, but will often ride the bow wave of boats and breach regularly. Occasionally, when swimming at high speed, Rough-toothed Dolphins hold their heads and chins above the surface of the water, in a characteristic behavior described as "skimming."

STATUS AND DISTRIBUTION: The Rough-toothed Dolphin has a worldwide distribution in tropical, subtropical and warm temperate waters, although its exact range remains poorly known. It is normally found in deep waters beyond the edge of the continental shelf. Rough-toothed Dolphins are extremely rare off the Pacific coast of the US and have stranded on only a few occasions. This dolphin occurs regularly from the Gulf of California southward into the eastern tropical Pacific, where water temperatures exceed 77°F (25°C). Here it is widespread at low densities, with the majority of sightings centered close to the equator.

Adult length: 6.8–8.5 ft (2.1–2.6 m)	**Group size:** Up to 50

1:33

Spinner Dolphin
Stenella longirostris

The most acrobatic of the dolphins.

IDENTIFICATION: There are several forms of Spinner Dolphin throughout the world and the details included below relate to the "eastern" race (*S. l. orientalis*), which is the only form to have been recorded regularly in the North American Pacific. The "eastern" Spinner Dolphin is a small, streamlined dolphin with a slim body, a gently sloping forehead and a long beak. The dorsal fin is tall and erect, the flippers are long and pointed and the tail flukes are swept back toward the tips. In mature males, the dorsal fin is often triangular in shape or angled slightly forward, giving the impression that the fin is positioned backward! Older males also develop a distinct anterior bulge under the tail stock, a feature that is clearly visible on leaping dolphins. The color of the body is uniform gray, with any light areas restricted to the throat and upper belly; there may also be light speckles on the belly. The beak is wholly dark and lacks the white tip of several other dolphin species.

SIMILAR SPECIES: Spinner Dolphins are similar in body shape and size to several other dolphin species in the North American Pacific, but at close range are easily distinguished by their long, slender beak and the triangular dorsal fin of adult males. No other dolphin is capable of hurling and twisting its body into the air in the way that a Spinner Dolphin can. The Pacific White-sided Dolphin (page 152) probably comes closest to mastering this skill, but is only able to rotate up to two times.

BEHAVIOR: The incredible spinning behavior of the Spinner Dolphins is one of the most acrobatic and energetic displays of any marine mammal. During a single vertical leap, which may exceed 10 feet (3 m) in height, a dolphin may twist through a 360° axis as many as seven times. It may also repeat such a leap up to 14 times in a row! Spinner Dolphins also regularly engage in spyhopping, head slapping, tail slapping, breaching, somersaults and tail stands. Although they frequently bow ride in other regions, in the eastern tropical Pacific they are usually cautious or nervous around boats. This is a highly gregarious species, generally occurring in very large pods and often associating with other dolphin species, particularly Pantropical Spotted Dolphins (page 142).

STATUS AND DISTRIBUTION: The Spinner Dolphin is widespread throughout the tropical to warm temperate waters of the world and is one of the commonest cetaceans in the tropics. In the North American Pacific, only the eastern race is present, and this is restricted to the warmest waters in the region. Eastern Spinner Dolphins occur in a roughly triangular section of the eastern tropical Pacific from central Baja California in the north to Ecuador in the south and approximately 145°W.

Adult length: 5–7.2 ft (1.5–2.2 m)	**Group size:** Up to 1,000

1:33

Pantropical Spotted Dolphin
Stenella attenuata

One of the most numerous dolphins on Earth.

IDENTIFICATION: The Pantropical Spotted Dolphin is a slim and streamlined dolphin with a falcate dorsal fin. The forehead slopes gently down to a relatively long beak. The flippers are sickle-shaped and the underside of the tail stock sometimes shows a pronounced keel. The species is most easily identified by its spotting, a feature that is unique amongst the cetaceans of the North American Pacific. However, at birth, the Pantropical Spotted Dolphin is unspotted and the body is distinctly two-toned—dark gray above and ivory beneath. As the dolphin matures, the skin darkens, with dark speckles appearing on the belly and pale spots on the upperside. With age, these spots increase in number and size and often merge. In adult Pantropical Spotted Dolphins, the dark dorsal fin and cape merge to lighter gray on the flanks and tail stock and to a pale gray belly. This gives the overall impression of a tricolored dolphin. In addition, a dark band runs horizontally along the upper mandible to the eye and another dark band extends from the beak to the dark flippers. The beak is dark with a white tip.

Globally there are several geographically distinct populations, which vary in size and coloration. Two of these, a nearshore form (*S. a. graffmani*) and an offshore form (*S. a. attenuata*), occur in the North American Pacific. The nearshore form is relatively large-bodied and heavily spotted, whereas the offshore form is smaller and generally less well-spotted.

SIMILAR SPECIES: The Pantropical Spotted Dolphin is very similar to the Short-beaked Common Dolphin (page 148), Long-beaked Common Dolphin (page 150) and Striped Dolphin (page 144) in shape, but lacks the strong flank markings and white belly of these species. The body coloration of young Pantropical Spotted Dolphins makes them almost indistinguishable from Common Bottlenose Dolphins (page 136). However, the presence of nearby adults should give away the species' identity.

BEHAVIOR: In coastal waters, Pantropical Spotted Dolphins generally occur in pods of less than 100, while offshore, pods of over 1,000 are not uncommon. The offshore form often associates with other dolphins, particularly Spinner Dolphins, as well as Yellowfin Tuna. Pantropical Spotted Dolphins enjoy riding bow waves and frequently engage in agile leaps and exuberant acrobatics.

STATUS AND DISTRIBUTION: The Pantropical Spotted Dolphin occurs throughout the world's oceans in tropical latitudes where surface water temperatures exceed 25°C, though it may also be found in subtropical to warm temperate waters. In the North American Pacific its regular range extends southward from the border between the US and Mexico to south of the equator. The coastal form, which generally occurs within 30 miles (50 km) of the shore, is present from the Gulf of California southward to northern Peru. The offshore form is present in tropical pelagic waters from central Mexico southward.

Adult length: 5.6–8.5 ft (1.7–2.6 m)   **Group size:** Generally 50–1,000

limit of nearshore form

1:33

Striped Dolphin
Stenella coeruleoalba

Predominantly found in offshore waters, where it can be abundant.

IDENTIFICATION: The Striped Dolphin is a slender species with a gently sloping forehead, prominent beak and a slightly hooked, triangular dorsal fin. The upper parts are dark gray, with a distinctive pale blaze that sweeps from the equally pale flank back and up toward the dorsal fin. A thin dark stripe runs along the lower flank from the eye to the underside of the tail stock, thickening toward the rear. This stripe can be difficult to see unless the dolphin jumps clear of the water. Another stripe, like a long eyelash, sweeps back from the eye and there is a further dark band that runs from the eye to the flipper. The underparts are white or pinkish.

SIMILAR SPECIES: In poor light or at long range, the Striped Dolphin can be quite difficult to distinguish from the Short-beaked Common Dolphin (page 148), Long-beaked Common Dolphin (page 150) and Pantropical Spotted Dolphin (page 142). All three species are broadly similar in size and shape and cannot be separated easily unless the patterning is observed. Confusion is also possible with Fraser's Dolphin (page 146), which is the only other dolphin in the region to possess a lateral stripe. However, two features in combination separate the Striped Dolphin from all other species: the distinctive lateral flank stripe and the pale blaze sweeping up beneath the dorsal fin.

BEHAVIOR: Striped Dolphins are very demonstrative, often seen leaping clear of the water or moving quickly toward the bow or wake of passing vessels. However, this behavior is observed less frequently in the North American Pacific than in many other parts of the world. Other regularly observed behaviors include tail slapping, head slapping and breaching. Pods vary greatly in size from less than ten to around 500, with an average of around 100.

STATUS AND DISTRIBUTION: The Striped Dolphin is distributed throughout the world in tropical, subtropical and warm temperate waters. It is generally pelagic, preferring deep water beyond the edge of the continental shelf. In the North American Pacific, the species occurs regularly as far north as California, where it is widespread and abundant in offshore waters. Farther north, the presence of Striped Dolphins is reflected by a small number of strandings in Oregon and Washington.

Adult length: 5.9–8.5 ft (1.8–2.6 m)	Group size: Up to 500

1:33

Fraser's Dolphin
Lagenodelphis hosei

Only discovered in the late 1950s and restricted to offshore tropical waters.

IDENTIFICATION: Fraser's Dolphin has a unique shape, being small and stocky with a short but distinct beak. The relatively small dorsal fin is almost triangular in shape and in males it can appear to be angled slightly forward. The flippers and flukes are also relatively small. The patterning and coloration of the body is highly characteristic, being bluish-gray above and pinkish-white below. A thick, dark stripe, often beginning as a "mask," extends from the eye and along the flank as far as the anus. This stripe becomes wider and darker with age, being least defined in juveniles and most striking in adult males. A pale cream-colored line runs from the forehead along the upper edge of the lateral flank stripe and a dark stripe runs between the base of the flipper and the lower jaw.

SIMILAR SPECIES: At a distance, the Fraser's Dolphin can be confused with other tropical oceanic dolphins of a similar size and shape, including both Long-beaked (page 150) and Short-beaked Common Dolphins (page 148), Striped Dolphin (page 144), Pantropical Spotted Dolphin (page 142), and Spinner Dolphin (page 140). However, the distinctive markings of the Fraser's Dolphin means that, in good light, confusion is only likely with the Striped Dolphin, which is less robust, has a larger dorsal fin, a longer beak, a thinner flank stripe and a pale dorsal blaze.

BEHAVIOR: Fraser's Dolphins generally occur in large pods of between 100 and 1,000, although much smaller groups are occasionally encountered. At the surface, these animals are often highly active, creating a burst of spray as they surface rapidly, often porpoising and breaching. Fraser's Dolphins are gregarious and frequently occur in mixed pods with several other species. Unlike many other dolphin species, Fraser's Dolphins rarely associate with seabirds or schools of tuna. This is because they generally feed at depths of over 650 feet (200 m). Although Fraser's Dolphins are known to approach vessels in other regions, this behavior is rare in the eastern tropical Pacific.

STATUS AND DISTRIBUTION: The status and distribution of Fraser's Dolphin remains poorly understood, but it occurs throughout the world and seems to be restricted to deep tropical waters. In the North American Pacific, the distribution of the species appears to be centered just north of the equator, with sightings ranging north as far as the southern tip of Baja California. With the exception of a few oceanic islands surrounded by deep water, Fraser's Dolphins rarely approach close to shore.

Adult length: 6.5–8.5 ft (2–2.6 m)	Group size: 100–1,000

1:33

Short-beaked Common Dolphin
Delphinus delphis

A fast and acrobatic swimmer that often relishes riding the bow waves of boats.

IDENTIFICATION: The Short-beaked Common Dolphin is a streamlined dolphin with a long, slender beak and a tall, falcate dorsal fin. The most striking identification feature is the characteristic "figure-eight" (∞) pattern on the flanks. At close range, the front half of the figure-eight appears tawny-yellow or brown and the rear half gray. The dark gray to black color of the upper back extends down into the central part of the figure-eight to form a distinctive point or 'V' directly below the dorsal fin. The belly is white. Close views also reveal that there is a thin black stripe extending from the flipper to the beak and a further dark stripe running from the eye to the beak. The base of the dorsal fin is often pale-centered.

SIMILAR SPECIES: The Short-beaked Common Dolphin is very similar in appearance to the Long-beaked Common Dolphin (page 150). The most obvious and striking difference is the length of the beak, but the Short-beaked Common Dolphin also has a shorter, stockier body, a more rounded forehead and a thinner dark line between the beak and the flipper. In addition, the demarcation between the dark back and pale flanks is more sharply defined than on the Long-beaked Common Dolphin. If seen distantly or in poor weather conditions, the Short-beaked Common Dolphin may be mistaken for other small dolphins such as the Striped Dolphin (page 144), Pantropical Spotted Dolphin (page 142) or Fraser's Dolphin (page 146). However, the distinctive flank pattern is the best way of distinguishing the Short-beaked Common Dolphin from these species.

BEHAVIOR: Short-beaked Common Dolphins are fast, energetic swimmers, readily attracted to the bow wave and wake of passing ships. This species is sometimes seen in large pods numbering thousands of animals. These pods may be highly active, porpoising at high speed and creating a lot of spray. Short-beaked Common Dolphins frequently associate with a number of other dolphin and whale species and usually feed close to the surface, often in the company of seabirds.

STATUS AND DISTRIBUTION: The Short-beaked Common Dolphin has a worldwide distribution in tropical, subtropical and temperate zones and is found both in shelf waters and beyond the edge of the continental shelf. In the North American Pacific, this is the most numerous dolphin in offshore warm temperate waters. Historically, sightings were rare north of central California. However, since 1990, following an El Niño event, a persistent period of warm water has allowed the Short-beaked Common Dolphin to become firmly established in this region where it has now become the most abundant cetacean. Farther south, the species remains common in Mexican waters and throughout the eastern tropical Pacific.

Adult length: 5.6–8.2 ft (1.7–2.5 m)	**Group size:** Generally up to 500

1:33

Long-beaked Common Dolphin
Delphinus capensis

Very similar to the Short-beaked Common Dolphin and only recognized as a separate species since 1992.

IDENTIFICATION: The Long-beaked Common Dolphin is a small, streamlined dolphin with striking body markings. The dorsal fin is generally tall and falcate, but its shape is highly variable and can be blunt or triangular. The beak is well-defined, relatively long and often dark with a white tip. Long-beaked Common Dolphins have a complex buff, gray and white criss-cross pattern on their flanks. The black dorsal fin often shows a pale center. The dark gray to black coloration of the upper back dips down to form a V-shape on the sides below the dorsal fin. The flanks are colored by complex swaths of yellowish-tan in front of the dorsal fin, changing to gray on the tail stock. The color and patterning on the flanks varies between individuals. The belly is white.

SIMILAR SPECIES: The Long-beaked Common Dolphin is easily distinguished from all but the Short-beaked Common Dolphin (page 148) by its distinctive figure-eight (∞) body pattern and striking yellow, gray and black coloration. It is very similar to the Short-beaked Common Dolphin, but is larger and has a longer beak and a more muted color pattern with a less crisp demarcation between the dark back and the pale flanks. It also has a less rounded and more flattened forehead, and a thicker dark line between the beak and the flipper.

BEHAVIOR: Long-beaked Common Dolphins are extremely active at the surface, where they spend much of the day traveling between feeding sites. They are inquisitive animals and will often change direction and travel a considerable distance to bow ride and leap in the wake of a fast-traveling boat or even a large whale. They are regularly observed performing a range of spectacular breaching maneuvers and tail slapping.

STATUS AND DISTRIBUTION: The Long-beaked Common Dolphin occurs throughout the tropical and warm temperate oceans of the world, although a historical lack of distinction between this species and the Short-beaked Common Dolphin means that outside the North American Pacific, little is known of its distribution. The ranges of both species frequently overlap and they may even be seen traveling together. Long-beaked Common Dolphins are common within a relatively narrow band of ocean approximately 50 miles (80 km) wide running between southern California to Baja California. They are also present throughout the Gulf of California. Their abundance varies from year to year and from season to season, probably due to changes in water temperature; it appears that the species moves northward during periods of warm water, perhaps explaining the population declines in Mexican waters during such periods.

Adult length: 5.6–8.2 ft (1.7–2.5 m)	**Group size:** Generally up to 500

1:33

Pacific White-sided Dolphin
Lagenorhynchus obliquidens

One of the commonest dolphins in the region.

IDENTIFICATION: The striking monochrome patterns, robust body shape and distinctive dorsal fin of the Pacific White-sided Dolphin make it difficult to confuse with any other small cetacean in the North American Pacific. The body of this dolphin is stocky, and the head tapers gently down to a small beak. The strongly curved dorsal fin is unusually large in comparison to the length of the body and its shape is unique among dolphins of a similar size, being perhaps most reminiscent of a female or immature Short-finned Pilot Whale (page 124).

SIMILAR SPECIES: The body pattern of the Pacific White-sided Dolphin is strikingly different from all other dolphins in the region. During rapid surfacing, they may superficially resemble the Dall's Porpoise (page 156), both species being contrastingly black and white in color, with two-tone dorsal fins. They are also both capable of producing a "rooster tail" spray, created as the head pushes quickly through the water. However, the much-smaller Dall's Porpoise has a low, triangular dorsal fin and is less demonstrative, tending not to leap clear of the water.

BEHAVIOR: The Pacific White-sided Dolphin is one of the most abundant and gregarious cetaceans in the North American Pacific. Pods of thousands may be encountered, although smaller groups of between 10 and 100 are more frequent. These pods often mix with other small cetaceans including Northern Right Whale Dolphins (page 154), Risso's Dolphins (page 134) and both species of common dolphin (pages 148 and 150), and are frequently found in close association with California Sea Lions (page 170) and seabirds. Pacific White-sided Dolphins are highly acrobatic and inquisitive animals capable of somersaults and breaching as many as 20 times in a single bout. They readily bow ride and particularly like to play in the wake of boats or to surf ocean waves. They are powerful swimmers and often create a "rooster tail" pattern of spray as they move rapidly at the surface.

STATUS AND DISTRIBUTION: The Pacific White-sided Dolphin occurs within a broad band across the North Pacific Ocean, preferring cold temperate waters to the south of Alaska and north of Baja California. It is most abundant in deep waters beyond the continental shelf, and is present close to land generally only in areas where deep-water channels occur nearshore. Seasonal movements tend to parallel movements of anchovy and other prey species. Between November and April, much of the northern population shifts southward, becoming most abundant in waters off California. Between May and October, as water temperatures increase, the population moves northward into Oregon, Washington and British Columbia, with animals present in the Gulf of Alaska during the warm summer months. The larger, southern population of this species occurs regularly off Baja California, extending as far south as the southwestern Gulf of California during the spring and summer months.

Adult length: 5.6–8.2 ft (1.7–2.5 m)　　　**Group size:** 10–100, infrequently 1,000 or more

1:33

Northern Right Whale Dolphin
Lissodelphis borealis

The only dolphin in the North American Pacific without a dorsal fin, this is one of the most bizarre-looking of all cetaceans.

IDENTIFICATION: The Northern Right Whale Dolphin is described by some as appearing "eel-like" in shape. It has a long slender body with a slim tail stock. The head is barely defined, having no prominent melon and only a small beak. At a distance, the species appears entirely black, although there are small areas of white on the belly, which are widest between the flippers and the tail stock, and there is a further white patch just behind the tip of the lower jaw. The tail flukes are dark gray on the upper surface and predominantly white underneath. Calves are lighter than adults, appearing light gray or cream-colored, but by the end of their first year their skin darkens to black.

SIMILAR SPECIES: Because the Northern Right Whale Dolphin lacks a dorsal fin, appears long and slim and often travels with low graceful leaps, it is more likely to be mistaken for a sea lion or fur seal than any cetacean. However, the unique shape and coloration of the Northern Right Whale Dolphin should readily distinguish it from all other marine mammals.

BEHAVIOR: The Northern Right Whale Dolphin is highly gregarious and regularly occurs in pods of over 100 and sometimes travels in groups of up to 3,000. It has also been observed associating with a wide range of other marine mammals. Northern Right Whale Dolphins have also been seen riding the pressure waves of large whales. They are not so playful around boats and are easily startled. However, they will bow ride, particularly when in the company of Pacific White-sided Dolphins. Northern Right Whale Dolphins are capable of speeds approaching 20 mph (30 km/h) and animals often leap in unison on a low, flat trajectory, working the sea into a froth as they move quickly at the surface in large groups. Pods often form into a V-shape, a chorus line or a compact group during travel. During high-speed movements, bellyflops, breaches and tail slapping are frequently observed.

STATUS AND DISTRIBUTION: The Northern Right Whale Dolphin is endemic to the temperate North Pacific Ocean, being generally restricted to seas between 30°N and 50°N. In the North American Pacific, it is present from British Columbia to Baja California, being found year-round in deep water beyond the edge of the continental shelf. During the fall, the population shifts southward and is found nearshore. In the winter it is regularly encountered as far south as southern California relatively close to the coast. In particularly cold water years, they probably range even farther south, occurring as far as Baja California. As water temperatures increase during the spring, Northern Right Whale Dolphins again head farther north and offshore.

Adult length: 6.6–10 ft (2–3.1 m)	**Group size:** Up to 500, sometimes more

1:33

Dall's Porpoise
Phocoenoides dalli

An exuberant cetacean found throughout much of the region.

IDENTIFICATION: The Dall's Porpoise is small and stout with a triangular dorsal fin and a distinctive surfacing style. It has a robust body and the head and tail flukes appear unusually small. The tail flukes are set behind a powerful tail stock with a bulge on the upper and lower sides. The flippers are small, rounded at the tip and located well forward on the body. Dall's Porpoises are predominantly black in color with a white tip to the dorsal fin. There is a large white patch on each flank directly below the dorsal fin, and these merge on the belly. Calves are dark gray on the upper side and light gray on the underside, becoming black and white as they mature. Their tail flukes are pointed at the tips and are dark. As the animal matures the color of the tail flukes changes and the trailing edge becomes white. The shape of the tail flukes also changes, becoming straight in females and convex and rounded in males.

SIMILAR SPECIES: Dall's Porpoise can be distinguished from the dolphins by its small size and the lack of a prominent beak. Confusion is possible with the Harbor Porpoise (page 158), but this species is uniformly gray and lacks the two-tone dorsal fin of Dall's Porpoise. Dall's Porpoises are generally far more energetic than Harbor Porpoises and its "rooster tail" surfacing behavior can be compared with that of the Pacific White-sided Dolphin (page 152), which is also capable of creating a similar spray pattern during rapid surfacing. However, these two species are quite different in structure and coloration.

BEHAVIOR: Dall's Porpoises are capable of high speeds of up to 35 mph (55 km/h). Darting and zigzagging behaviors are typical as they race toward a fast-moving boat to ride the bow wave or play in the wake. Dall's Porpoises often move rapidly and powerfully through the water creating a distinctive pattern of white spray known as a "rooster tail." Pod sizes are generally between 2 and 20, although several hundred have been known to congregate on feeding banks off Alaska. Dall's Porpoise is predominantly a nocturnal hunter and is often seen at rest during the day. They are regularly seen in close proximity to several other species of whale and dolphin.

STATUS AND DISTRIBUTION: Dall's Porpoise is restricted to a broad band across the North Pacific where surface water temperatures range between 37° and 64°F (3°–18°C). In the North American Pacific, it is one of the most abundant small cetaceans between Alaska and California, extending as far south as Baja California in cold years. It is widespread in both nearshore and offshore waters. Although some populations are probably resident, latitudinal and nearshore–offshore movements are known to occur in some regions.

Adult length: 5.6–7.2 ft (1.7–2.2 m)	**Group size:** 2–20

1:33

Harbor Porpoise
Phocoena phocoena

A diminutive cetacean regularly seen in northern parts of the region.

IDENTIFICATION: The Harbor Porpoise has a robust body and a small, rounded head that lacks a beak. The centrally positioned dorsal fin is small, low and triangular with a blunt tip. The upper parts of the body are dark gray, merging to lighter gray on the flanks, and the underside is light gray to white. Calves and juveniles tend to have brownish backs.

SIMILAR SPECIES: The Harbor Porpoise may be confused with its near relative the Dall's Porpoise (page 156), particularly in poor light when the striking black-and-white coloration of the latter species may be indistinguishable. However, the Harbor Porpoise lacks the pale-tipped black dorsal fin and does not exhibit the fast, active behavior of Dall's Porpoise. Although Harbor Porpoises share their lethargic behavior, gray coloration and lack of a distinctive beak with both the Dwarf (page 100) and Pygmy Sperm Whales (page 98), their distributions do not generally overlap. On surfacing, the Harbor Porpoise can be distinguished from both of the small Sperm Whales as it arches its back higher above the water, revealing a dorsal fin that is large in relation to its body length. This leaves the observer with the impression that the fin is rotating on a wheel as the body rolls forward. At long range, the Harbor Porpoise may be confused with the much larger Common Bottlenose Dolphin (page 136), which also shows a centrally positioned dorsal fin and uniform gray upper parts. However, when seen well, the diminutive size, uniform coloration, triangular shape of the dorsal fin and unobtrusive behavior should distinguish the Harbor Porpoise from all other small cetaceans in the region.

BEHAVIOR: Harbor Porpoises generally live alone or in small groups and travel quite slowly. They are unobtrusive and very difficult to observe in rough weather. Unlike many dolphin species, this species is shy and rarely approaches boats; indeed they often move away from vessels. While feeding, animals usually surface slowly three or four times before diving for a duration of two to three minutes. Logging is occasionally observed, when the porpoise sometimes sweeps its head from side to side while the body remains motionless at the surface. Exuberant activity is rare.

STATUS AND DISTRIBUTION: The Harbor Porpoise is restricted to the cold temperate to subarctic oceans of the northern hemisphere. Predominantly a coastal species, it favors waters nearshore of the 656-foot (200-m) depth contour. In the North American Pacific, the Harbor Porpoise is one of the most widespread and abundant coastal cetaceans from central California northward to Alaska. Although nearshore-offshore and north-south movements may occur in some populations, others are known to be resident. The population has declined significantly in the last 30 years due to increased levels of pollution, loss of prey through overfishing and accidental capture in bottom-set fishing nets.

Adult length: 4.9–5.9 ft (1.5–1.8 m)	**Group size:** Up to 10, sometimes more

1:33

Vaquita
Phocoena sinus

The smallest cetacean with the most restricted range, and one of the rarest species in the world.

IDENTIFICATION: The Vaquita is the smallest cetacean of all. Like other members of its family, it has a robust body shape, a centrally positioned dorsal fin and a cone-shaped head lacking a prominent beak. The dorsal fin is almost triangular in shape and is tall when compared with other porpoise species, the front edge curving backward toward the tip and the rear edge being straight and vertical. The body appears gray, graduating to paler toward the belly. Immature animals are darker but become a more uniform pale gray as they mature. However, they generally retain some dark coloration on the underside of the tail stock and around the eye, lip and chin and often develop a dark stripe from the chin to the flipper.

SIMILAR SPECIES: Although the Vaquita is similar in appearance to several other small cetaceans, including the Harbor Porpoise (page 158), Dwarf Sperm Whale (page 100) and Pygmy Sperm Whale (page 98), it is unlikely to be confused with any of them due to its restricted and isolated geographical range. This species' distribution is separated from that of its close relative, the Harbor Porpoise, by the Baja peninsula. The most likely confusion species within its range is the Common Bottlenose Dolphin (page 136) but this is much larger and has a prominent beak, generally occurs in larger groups and is far more energetic and acrobatic.

BEHAVIOR: The Vaquita's surfacing sequence is distinctive. The animal surfaces slowly, barely disturbing the water around it. An indistinct blow may be observed and a sharp, puffing sound, reminiscent of the Harbor Porpoise, heard. As the robust body rolls forward, a prominent shark-like dorsal fin appears. The animal usually disappears quickly, denying onlookers a second opportunity of a sighting. Observations at sea suggest that the Vaquita is a very shy animal that tends to avoid boats. When undisturbed it swims and feeds in a leisurely manner, rolling slowly at the surface. Sightings generally involve single animals or small groups of two to four, although groups of up to 10 have occasionally been seen.

STATUS AND DISTRIBUTION: The Vaquita has the most restricted range of any marine cetacean in the world, occurring only in a small region of the northwestern Gulf of California where its distribution is centered in the shallow coastal waters close to the mouth of the Colorado River. The majority of sightings come from waters adjacent to San Felipe, Rocas Consag and El Golfo de Santa Clara, where the species is highly localized and probably resident. All of the sightings have been in shallow coastal waters less than 130 feet (40 m) deep and up to 16 miles (25 km) from shore. This species has declined to the brink of extinction with the current population estimated at just 500 animals.

Adult length: 3.9–4.9 ft (1.2–1.5 m)	**Group size:** Up to 4, occasionally up to 10

1:33

QUICK REFERENCE GUIDE
Seals, Sea Lions and the Sea Otter

Scale 1:25

Northern Fur Seal female
4.6 ft (1.4 m)
PAGE 164

Northern Fur Seal male
6.9 ft (2.1 m)
PAGE 164

Guadalupe Fur Seal female
3.9 ft (1.2 m)
PAGE 166

Guadalupe Fur Seal male
5.9 ft (1.8 m)
PAGE 166

California Sea Lion female
6.6 ft (2 m)
PAGE 170

California Sea Lion male
7.9 ft (2.4 m)
PAGE 170

Steller Sea Lion female
6.2 ft (1.9 m)
PAGE 168

Steller Sea Lion male
7.9 ft (2.4 m)
PAGE 168

Northern Elephant Seal male
13.5 ft (4.1 m)
PAGE 172

Northern Elephant Seal female
9.8 ft (3 m)
PAGE 172

Harbor Seal
4.6–6.2 ft (1.4–1.9 m) male
3.9–5.6 ft (1.2–1.7 m) female
PAGE 174

mon Bottlenose Dolphin
ft (3 m) for comparison

Sea Otter
4.9 ft (1.5 m) male
4.6 ft (1.4 m) female
PAGE 176

2   4   6 feet

163

Northern Fur Seal
Callorhinus ursinus

This species is among the most pelagic of all pinnipeds, spending up to 11 months of the year at sea.

IDENTIFICATION: The Northern Fur Seal is a robust species, adult males being considerably larger than females. Both sexes have a relatively small head and a short, pointed muzzle, giving a characteristic profile, and the hind flippers are very long. They have long, dense whiskers and long external ear flaps. Adult males are dark brown to black, with gray guard hairs on the back of the mane. Females and subadults have a silvery-gray back and reddish-brown underparts. Pups are mainly black at birth, with a white or silvery belly, chest and face.

SIMILAR SPECIES: The Northern Fur Seal is much smaller than either California (page 170) or Steller Sea Lions (page 168) of the same age and sex, and has relatively longer whiskers. The Guadalupe Fur Seal (page 166) is smaller, lighter brown and has a relatively larger head and longer, more pointed muzzle. Juveniles are very difficult to tell apart from juvenile sea lions and Guadalupe Fur Seals.

BEHAVIOR: At sea, adult Northern Fur Seals are usually seen alone or in pairs, but sometimes in groups of three or more. They are highly gregarious during the breeding season when very large numbers gather at rookeries. Adult males begin to arrive at the rookeries in May and establish territories that may eventually hold several females. The pregnant females begin to arrive in mid-June and give birth within a few days of arrival; mating occurs five or six days after pupping. Pupping continues until early August and the pup is weaned after about four months, following which the adult female leaves the rookery to migrate south. The males leave the breeding islands from August to October. Outside the breeding season both sexes spend long periods at sea.

STATUS AND DISTRIBUTION: The Northern Fur Seal occurs from the Bering Sea south to San Miguel Island off southern California. During the breeding season approximately three quarters of the world population is found in the Pribilof Islands of St. George and St. Paul in the southern Bering Sea, with the remaining animals spread throughout the North Pacific. Of the seals in the North American Pacific, outside the Pribilofs, less than 1% of the population is found off San Miguel Island, California. Northern Fur Seals may temporarily haul out on land at other sites in Alaska, British Columbia and on islets along the coast of the continental US, but usually outside the breeding season. Northern Fur Seals have been very heavily exploited since the 18th century and it is estimated that several million animals were killed for their luxurious pelts. The world population is currently estimated at 1.1 million animals, but has been declining since the late 1950s.

Adult length: Male 6.9 ft (2.1 m); female 4.6 ft (1.4 m)

1:25

Guadalupe Fur Seal
Arctocephalus townsendi

The least well-known seal in the region, having recovered from the brink of extinction.

IDENTIFICATION: The Guadalupe Fur Seal is the smallest of the eared seals in the North American Pacific. Adult males have a robust head, shoulders and neck, with a more slender rear torso. Females are smaller and slimmer, with a more evenly proportioned head and torso. Both sexes have a long, narrow, pointed snout. The fore flippers are large and the hind flippers relatively short compared with other fur seals. Bulls have long guard hairs extending from the back of the head to the lower chest, forming a distinct, uniform mane. The pelage of both sexes ranges from dark grayish-brown to dusky-black. On males, the tips of the guard hairs on the mane may be buff, giving much of the head and neck an overall tan appearance.

SIMILAR SPECIES: Guadalupe Fur Seals may very occasionally occur with Northern Fur Seals (page 164) in the Channel Islands off California and can be separated from this species by their longer, more pointed snout, smaller hind flippers and larger fore flippers. However, unaccompanied juveniles are more difficult to identify. The species may overlap with the California Sea Lion (page 170) off southern California and the coast of Baja California. Juvenile and adult female animals can be separated from California Sea Lions by their darker pelages and slimmer, more pointed snouts. Adult males can be distinguished from bull California Sea Lions by their smaller size, longer snout and lack of a sagittal crest.

BEHAVIOR: The Guadalupe Fur Seal is one of the least-known seals in the North American Pacific. Individual males mate with several females during a single breeding season. In early June, males establish territories along rocky coastlines. Females give birth to a single pup from early June to early August and mate about a week after giving birth. The pups stay with their mothers for eight to ten months. While ashore, Guadalupe Fur Seals are less social than other seals. In nearshore waters they spend considerable periods grooming at the water's edge or resting in tidal pools to keep cool. Another cooling-off behavior involves hanging almost motionless in the water with the head pointed toward the seabed and the hind flippers protruding just above the surface. Outside the breeding season they are largely solitary and spend long periods at sea.

STATUS AND DISTRIBUTION: The Guadalupe Fur Seal was heavily exploited by sealers until the early 20th century, when it was considered extinct. In 1954, 14 individuals were discovered on Guadalupe Island off Baja California. Following protection measures, the population has grown to over 10,000. The breeding range of the Guadalupe Fur Seal is restricted almost exclusively to Guadalupe Island, although researchers recently discovered another small rookery at San Benito Island off Baja California. Outside the breeding season they wander as far north as central California and south to the Gulf of California.

Adult length: Male 5.9 ft (1.8 m); female 3.9 ft (1.2 m)

1:25

Steller Sea Lion
Eumetopias jubatus

The largest of the eared seals in the region.

IDENTIFICATION: The Steller Sea Lion has a robust torso and head, short blunt snout and characteristically large fore flippers. The hind flippers are short and slim. The bulls are considerably larger than adult females, especially around the head, shoulders and neck. Adult males have an obvious forehead and a distinctive mane of long hairs extending from the back of the neck down the shoulders and chest. Both sexes are colored light to reddish-brown, with most of the underparts and flippers dark brown to black. Pups are blackish-brown at birth, molting to a blonder pelage at around six months old.

SIMILAR SPECIES: Steller Sea Lion can be readily distinguished from both Northern Fur Seal (page 164) and California Sea Lion (page 170) by its substantially larger body and massive head and shoulders. Compared with Northern Fur Seals, Steller Sea Lions have a paler pelage and proportionately shorter hind flippers.

BEHAVIOR: Steller Sea Lions gather together on rocky shorelines in moderate-sized groups during the summer breeding season and again in the fall and winter, when they molt. The bulls arrive at the breeding colonies in early May and establish territories using visual and vocal displays. The females arrive slightly later and give birth to a single pup that is weaned by the age of one. Animals tend to be more widely separated from one another at the rookeries during the breeding season than at other times of the year. At sea, Steller Sea Lions form large groups that appear to consist of females of all ages and subadult males; adult males are usually found alone. Steller Sea Lions are not known to migrate, but they do disperse widely outside the breeding season. Foraging trips vary with age, sex and season. In the summer, when females are attending young pups, foraging trips average 10 miles (17 km) and last up to 25 hours. In winter, when the pups are older, foraging trips average 80 miles (130 km) and last for up to 200 hours.

STATUS AND DISTRIBUTION: The Steller Sea Lion is restricted to coastal waters of the North Pacific Rim, stretching from northern Japan to California. In the North American Pacific they breed in numerous rookeries in the Gulf of Alaska and British Columbia, with smaller numbers in Oregon south to Año Nuevo Island off central California. Since the 1980s, numbers have declined by over 90% in much of Alaska and California. However, populations in Oregon, British Columbia and southeast Alaska have remained stable or have increased slightly. In 1994, the total world population of this endangered species was estimated at approximately 100,000, of which 30% breed in the North American Pacific.

Adult length: Male 7.9 ft (2.4 m); female 6.2 (1.9 m)

1:25

California Sea Lion
Zalophus californianus

The most familiar and commonly seen sea lion in the region.

IDENTIFICATION: The sexes of California Sea Lion are very different in size, with bulls weighing up to four times more than adult females. Adult males have a particularly robust head and neck, with a more slender rear torso; adult females and juveniles have more uniformly slender bodies. Both sexes have a long, narrow snout, with the males having a pronounced forehead and pale sagittal crest. They have long fore flippers and relatively short hind flippers. Adult males are predominantly dark chestnut-brown, but can range from pale brown to black. Adult females and juveniles are blonde to tan, and newborn pups dark brown to black.

SIMILAR SPECIES: In the northern part of its range, the California Sea Lion overlaps with the Steller Sea Lion (page 168) and Northern Fur Seal (page 164). However, it is considerably smaller and less robust than the Steller Sea Lion and lacks its characteristic mane. It also has slimmer fore flippers than Steller Sea Lion and is consistently darker. California Sea Lions can be distinguished from Northern Fur Seals by their larger size, slimmer fore flippers and longer snout. In the south of its range the California Sea Lion may also overlap with Guadalupe Fur Seal (page 166), but is larger and more robust, with a longer snout. The males of both species of fur seal lack the prominent forehead and pale crest of California Sea Lion.

BEHAVIOR: California Sea Lions are regularly found resting on breakwaters, harbors and boats. They are highly gregarious and gather ashore in large groups of up to several thousand individuals. When at sea they also travel, forage and socialize in groups numbering tens or even hundreds of animals. California Sea Lions form large rookeries on sandy beaches and rocky islands during the breeding season. Adult males arrive at breeding sites in early May and establish territories using visual threat displays and frequent barking. Pregnant females come ashore between May and July and give birth to a single pup. The pup is weaned after 6 to 12 months. When foraging, dives typically last for two minutes, but can be as long as 10 minutes, with animals readily seizing fish from commercial fishing nets and lines.

STATUS AND DISTRIBUTION: The range of California Sea Lion extends from southern British Columbia south to central Mexico. The main breeding colonies include the Channel Islands in southern California and several islands off the coast of Baja California. Outside the breeding season, large numbers, principally males, migrate north, both within the Gulf of California, and along the Pacific Coast as far as Vancouver Island. Hunting in the 19th century drastically reduced the population of California Sea Lions, with only 1,500 animals surviving by 1920. Following protection, they have made a remarkable recovery and the world population is now estimated to be between 211,000 and 241,000.

Adult length: Male 7.9 ft (2.4 m); female 6.6 ft (2 m)

1:25

Northern Elephant Seal
Mirounga angustirostris

A massive and spectacular species, and the largest seal found in the region.

IDENTIFICATION: The sexes of Northern Elephant Seal are very different in size, with the bulls being up to four times heavier than adult females. This is a very robustly built, long-bodied seal with a very large head and proportionately short fore flippers. As males mature they develop a chest "shield"—a thick-skinned region of the neck and shoulders that becomes pitted and heavily scarred during territorial fights. Adult males have a distinctive, elongated, fleshy snout or proboscis. Females and juveniles have a more rounded head, shorter hind flippers and no proboscis. Adult females and juveniles are colored buff to deep brown on the upper side, yellowing to tan on the underside. Adult males are uniformly dark brown throughout except for the neck area, which is speckled with pink and white.

SIMILAR SPECIES: Adult Northern Elephant Seals are readily distinguished from all other pinnipeds in the North American Pacific by their large size and by the fleshy nose of adult males. Away from breeding and molting sites, their solitary, pelagic habits mean that it is unlikely they will be seen with any other species of seal.

BEHAVIOR: Northern Elephant Seals are highly pelagic, spending over three-quarters of their lives at sea and only coming ashore for short periods to breed and molt. While at sea they are usually found alone and spend as much as 90% of their time submerged. Adult males appear to spend more time foraging in waters over the continental shelf, while females spend long periods in deeper, open waters. Unlike other pinnipeds, Northern Elephant Seals are shy and are not easily approached by boats. They breed from December to March, when up to several hundred animals may haul out together on sand or gravel beaches. Dominant bulls preside over groups of females and competition between males can be intense, leading to spectacular, bloody contests. The females have a single pup that is nursed for about a month before being weaned abruptly. Following mating, the females leave the beaches, returning in late April or May to molt. Males return to land to molt later in the year between May and August.

STATUS AND DISTRIBUTION: Confined to the North American Pacific, Northern Elephant Seals were intensively hunted until the end of the 19th century, by which time only a handful survived. Following full protection, the population has increased steadily and today numbers in excess of 150,000 animals. At least two-thirds of the breeding population occurs in the Channel Islands off southern California. Other colonies occur at the Farallon and Año Nuevo islands off central California and along the central California mainland. Colonies also exist on Guadalupe, San Benito and Cedros islands. Outside the breeding season, females range in pelagic waters off Oregon and Washington, while males migrate as far north as the Gulf of Alaska.

Adult length: Male 13.5 ft (4.1 m); female 9.8 ft (3 m)

1:40

Harbor Seal
Phoca vitulina

A non-migratory species occurring predominantly in coastal waters throughout much of the region.

IDENTIFICATION: The Harbor Seal is one of the smallest seals inhabiting the North American Pacific. They have small fore flippers and lack the external ear flaps typical of fur seals and sea lions. The Harbor Seal has a relatively small head with a short, concave, dog-like muzzle. The eyes are relatively large and close-set, and the nostrils look V-shaped when viewed head-on. The color and pattern of the coat is highly variable, ranging from light to dark gray, brown or reddish and with a covering of dark spots or pale, ring-like markings. The belly is usually lighter with reduced blotching. The pups shed their whitish lanugo (downy hair) within 10 days after their birth, thereafter resembling adults in coloration.

SIMILAR SPECIES: The small size and characteristic mottled coat should distinguish the Harbor Seal from all other pinnipeds in the North American Pacific.

BEHAVIOR: At sea the Harbor Seal is usually found alone or in small groups, generally occurring nearshore and only occasionally being seen in pelagic waters. It is gregarious on land and prefers to haul out on sandy estuaries, intertidal sandbanks, rocky shorelines and drifting glacial ice. When hauled out on shore, groups often lie with their heads and hind flippers elevated in a characteristic "banana-like" posture. When diving this species sinks below the surface (like Elephant Seals) rather than porpoising clear of the water (like the eared seals). In spring and early summer, female Harbor Seals come ashore and give birth to a single pup. The pup is well developed at birth and must be able to swim just a few hours later to ensure that it survives the following tide. Males play no part in raising the pups and spend most of the time offshore from the rookeries.

STATUS AND DISTRIBUTION: The Harbor Seal is the most widely distributed pinniped in the world, inhabiting temperate and subarctic coastal areas on both sides of the North Pacific and North Atlantic Oceans. In the North American Pacific, it is found in coastal waters from the Gulf of Alaska to Baja California. It is generally non-migratory, with local movements associated with such factors as tides, weather conditions, food availability and breeding. Prior to being afforded protection in the 1970s, the population of Harbor Seals along the west coast of North America was greatly reduced by commercial hunting. In the last 40 years the population along the coasts of California, Oregon and British Columbia has increased significantly. However, there has been a population decline in the Gulf of Alaska within the last 20 to 30 years. It is estimated that the current total population of Harbor Seals in the eastern North Pacific is 285,000.

Adult length: Male 4.6–6.2 ft (1.4–1.9 m); female 3.9–5.6 ft (1.2–1.7 m)

1:25

Sea Otter
Enhydra lutris

One of the most familiar marine mammals of the North American Pacific.

IDENTIFICATION: The Sea Otter has a broad head and short, blunt muzzle covered with whiskers. The hind feet are large, flattened and flipper-like; the fore feet short and rounded. The tail is long, horizontally flattened and untapered. Unlike cetaceans and pinnipeds, Sea Otters lack a layer of blubber, but are kept warm by a coat of sparse guard hairs and dense underfur. In adults, the fur is pale brown to black and the guard hairs can be dark or blonde. The head and neck become paler with age, with some older animals having entirely white faces. Juveniles are generally dark brown, while pups are fawn-colored at birth.

SIMILAR SPECIES: The Sea Otter is only likely to be confused with the River Otter. However, they can be readily distinguished from River Otters by their large, flipper-like hind feet and flattened tail. Their behavior is also a useful method of separating these two species: Sea Otters swim predominantly on their backs, while River Otters generally swim on their stomachs.

BEHAVIOR: Sea Otters spend most of their lives in the sea, usually within several feet of the shore, occasionally hauling out on land. They spend considerable lengths of time afloat on their backs when sleeping, grooming or eating captured prey. Although Sea Otters are not particularly gregarious, females sometimes form loose groups numbering up to 20, while bachelor male groups can number up to several hundred, sometimes as floating "rafts" attached to kelp beds. Individual males mate with several females usually during the summer and fall. The female gives birth to a single pup that is nursed between six months and a year. Sea Otters predominantly forage in coastal waters up to 160 ft (50 m) deep. An interesting aspect of their foraging behavior is the use of small rocks as tools, which they hold in their paws to break the exoskeletons of their invertebrate prey.

STATUS AND DISTRIBUTION: Sea Otters are confined to nearshore waters of the North Pacific Rim from California northward along the coast to the Gulf of Alaska, through the Aleutian Islands to northern Japan. They were abundant throughout their range until the middle of the 18th century but were then very heavily exploited by furriers. By 1911, when they were afforded protection, only a few thousand remained. They have since recovered throughout most of their range, in part aided by several reintroduction programs. In the 1990s the Alaskan population was estimated at 100,000, but there have been some marked declines in the last decade. In California, the population currently numbers about 1,700, concentrated from Monterey Bay to Point Conception.

Adult length: Male 4.9 ft (1.5 m); female 4.6 ft (1.4 m)

1:25

Whale-watching in the North American Pacific

Commercial whale-watching in North America dates from a winter's day in 1955 when a Californian fisherman, Chuck Chamberlin, offered the public a trip to watch migrating Gray Whales for a fee of just one dollar. Interest in the whales grew gradually and by the mid 1970s the annual migration of Gray Whales had captured the public's imagination and whale-watching spread rapidly along the entire coastline of the North American Pacific. As interest gathered, trips expanded to include other species of whales and dolphins, along with other marine mammals such as seals and sea lions.

The whale-watching craze rapidly spread to the Eastern Seaboard of Canada the US and then around the world. Today, the whale-watching industry generate excess of US$1 billion per year and has one of the fastest growth rates of any for tourism in North America and around the world.

The annual migration of Gray Whales from their breeding grounds on Pacific Coast of Baja to their feeding grounds off Alaska still forms the main of the whale-watching industry in the North American Pacific. However, increa populations of other great whales, such as Humpbacks and Blues, now regu visit waters of the nearshore North American Pacific, and good numbers of sm cetaceans are being encountered more frequently as boats venture farther offs and new feeding areas are discovered.

With a bit of luck and perseverance several species of marine mammals be seen almost anywhere along the coast of the North American Pacific, bu largest numbers and greatest variety are fou five main areas: Baja and the Gu California, the Cha Islands, Central Califo British Columbia Washington Southeast Al

Tourists watching a Gray Whale mother and calf

Baja and the Gulf of California

Gray Whales have been coming to the pristine waters of the San Ignacio lagoons along the Pacific coast of Baja for thousands of years to breed and bear their young. Close interactions with people in the breeding lagoons offer a wilderness experience that many visitors have described as life-changing. The phenomenon began in the 1960s when, for whatever reason, mother Gray Whales brought their calves over and "introduced" them first to local fishermen and research boats, and now to tourists.

The breeding season lasts from late December to March and whale-watching trips to the lagoons can be arranged as part of a one- or two-week-long trip from San Diego in a self-contained boat. Alternatively, land-based whale-watchers can stay in safari-like campsites around Magdalena Bay or San Ignacio Lagoon, and are then taken out in small Mexican boats called "pangas" to encounter the whales.

The Gulf of California, also known as the Sea of Cortez, has year-round populations of Bryde's, Fin, Humpback and Blue Whales. It is also an excellent area to encounter large numbers of dolphins—several species are represented, but the most commonly encountered are Short- and Long-beaked Common, Pacific White-sided and Common Bottlenose. To see cetaceans in the Gulf of California, most travelers take a one- or two-week cruise boat from La Paz or San Diego.

The Channel Islands

From February to May more than 20,000 Gray Whales migrate through the 25-mile-wide (40-km) strait between Santa Barbara and the Channel Islands. The migratory route is easily accessed by boats that leave daily from the Santa Barbara waterfront from late winter through early summer. The trips are relatively short, averaging two to three hours, because the whales are often close to shore, sometimes in the kelp beds. Gray Whales are not the only whales to frequent the channel. During the late spring and summer months, good numbers of Humpback and Blue Whales visit the waters around the Channel Islands to gorge on the vast shoals of krill and baitfish that congregate there. The Humpbacks are present from late April onwards, while the Blues arrive in late June, remaining until October. The trips to see Humpbacks and Blues are full-day affairs leaving at around 8 a.m. and returning at 3 p.m.

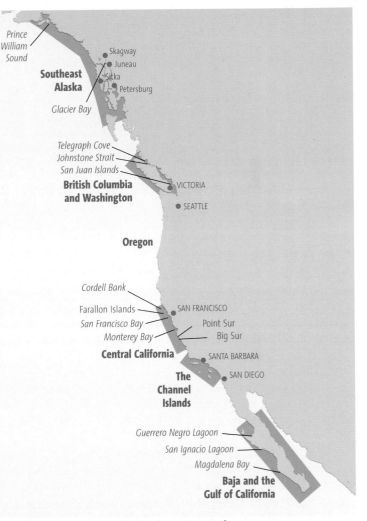

Principal whale-watching areas in the North American Pacific

For a closer encounter with these gentle giants, boat trips depart from many ports along this stretch of coast. Major whale-watching centers include the ports of Monterey, Santa Cruz, San Francisco and Bodega Bay.

From May to December boats also sail to the marine sanctuaries of Monterey Bay, the Farallon Islands and the Cordell Bank. The trips usually last 6–10 hours and regularly encounter several species of whales, along with good numbers of dolphins and pinnipeds. Of the great whales, Humpbacks are the most regularly seen, but Blues are often encountered, along with smaller numbers of Fin and Common Minke Whales. The most frequently sighted dolphins include Pacific White-sided, Short-beaked Common and Risso's. Northern Right Whale Dolphins and Long-beaked Common Dolphins are also regularly seen, particularly during the fall and winter months. Sometimes the dolphins travel in spectacular pods of several thousand.

British Columbia and Washington

The coastline of British Columbia and Washington has become synonymous with one species of cetacean in particular—the Killer Whale or Orca. Thousands of whale-watchers from North America and throughout the world travel to this region primarily to encounter this charismatic species.

Killer Whales are found year-round in the Pacific Northwest, particularly favoring the inlets and sheltered waterways around the US–Canada border area. It is possible to see Killer Whales almost anywhere throughout this region—from shore, ferry, cruise ship or dedicated whale-watch boat. However, the best chance of encountering this species is in two principal locations: Johnstone Strait off northeast Vancouver Island and around the San Juan Islands. A large proportion of the whale-watch boats that visit Johnstone Strait depart from the small coastal town of Telegraph Cove, while most boats for the San Juan Islands leave from Victoria. Other cetacean species such as Humpback and Common Minke Whales, Pacific White-sided Dolphins and Dall's and Harbor Porpoises are also regularly seen on these trips.

The best time to see Killer Whales is from June to September. Migrating Gray Whales are also seen off Vancouver in March and April. In the autumn

In addition to the great whales, a variety of porpoises and dolphins are abundant in these waters. Those most regularly encountered include Long- and Short-beaked Common, Pacific White-sided and Risso's Dolphins. Northern Right Whale Dolphins and Dall's Porpoises are also seen, though infrequently. Sightings of Harbor Seals and California Sea Lions are commonplace, while Northern Elephant Seals and Steller Sea Lions are spotted with some regularity.

Central California

The coastline of central and northern California offers some outstanding land-based lookout spots for watching migrating Gray Whales. The Grays are sometimes only a few hundred feet offshore in the surf or giant kelp beds. The best time to look for the whales is during the northward spring migration when they move closer to shore. Some of the best-known vantage points include Point Reyes, just north of San Francisco, Pigeon Point Lighthouse near Santa Cruz and Point Lobos just south of Monterey. The 75-mile-long (120 km) Big Sur coastline has many promontories along its length, which make excellent vantage points for viewing the migrating whales.

and winter, cetacean sightings decline, but for the marine mammal enthusiast the rugged coast of the Pacific Northwest becomes home to large numbers of pinnipeds. Every fall about 3,000 California Sea Lions migrate north to join up with 8,000 Steller Sea Lions that have dispersed from their northern rookeries. The sea lions often congregate on reefs, beaches and log booms along with Harbor Seals and flocks of Bald Eagles, where they feast on herring and other small fish.

Southeast Alaska

With a backdrop of snow-covered peaks, lush evergreen forests and calving glaciers, and over 15 species of cetaceans plying its waters, Alaska offers some of the most spectacular whale watching in the world.

Summer is the whale-watching season in southeast Alaska, when the weather and sea conditions are calmest. Summer is also the best time for whales. Large numbers of Humpback Whales that winter off Hawaii migrate to Alaskan waters where they spend the summer and fall gorging on huge shoals of herring and candlefish. In addition, smaller numbers of Fin, Common Minke and Killer Whales are regularly seen. Of the smaller cetaceans, Dall's and Harbor Porpoises are common and Pacific White-sided Dolphins are occasionally encountered. Rocky islets hold small colonies of Harbor Seals and Steller Sea Lions, while the shorelines of southern Alaska are among the best locations in North America to find Sea Otters.

Whales and dolphins can be encountered almost anywhere in this region, but two of the premier locations are Glacier Bay and Prince William Sound. Increasing numbers of whale-watching trips are being offered from Gustavus, Petersburg, Juneau, Valdez and Sitka, as well as other small towns. Most trips are on small fishing boats or medium-sized motorboats and last for three to six hours.

Another premier location to see whales is Alaska's "Inside Passage." This marine highway runs for nearly 375 miles (600 km) from the Alaska–British Columbia border north to the port of Skagway. Many cruise ships and passenger ferries ply these waters throughout the summer and offer excellent opportunities to encounter whales and dolphins. Both cruise ships and ferries will regularly make deviations to get closer looks at whales and other marine wildlife. For the more brave and adventurous, some operators offer kayak trips and an unparalleled opportunity to observe whales up close and at sea level.

A Spectacular Day in the Sea of Cortez

Todd Pusser

Trying to narrow down one spectacular day of whale-watching in the Sea of Cortez is next to impossible. I have spent a good deal of time on the water in this magnificent sea and have had numerous banner days with cetaceans. So many wonderful memories come to mind. I recall that hot summer day in early August off San Felipe in the northern Sea of Cortez when I saw my first Vaquita, one of the world's most endangered cetaceans and certainly the most endangered species of porpoise. I recall the rate at which my pulse quickened and my respiration became shallow as a pair of Vaquita rolled slowly at the surface just 300 feet (100 m) from the ship I was standing on. I remember thinking that I may never see that species again. Little did I know that I would eventually have eight sightings of twelve different Vaquitas later that same day!

Or perhaps it was the time I observed a group of eight Killer Whales harassing a pair of Fin Whales just north of the Midriff Islands. Watching the Fin Whales porpoise through the water at an almost unbelievable rate toward the horizon with the Killers in pursuit certainly ranks as one of my most memorable cetacean encounters. Or maybe it was the day we encountered a lone Sperm Whale offshore of Guaymas, Mexico, in the eastern Sea of Cortez that was entangled in a gillnet. Emaciated and near death, the whale could barely surface to breathe as the weight of the net that wrapped around the mid-body and tail stock hampered its movements. Speaking of Sperm Whales, on a more lively note, I remember a pair of them breaching simultaneously over and over again offshore of Loreto.

I recall my first Blue Whale encounter in the Sea of Cortez almost like it was yesterday. We were just offshore of La Paz and had encountered numerous Fin Whales lunge feeding in one small area when a whale popped up in the group with the unmistakable mottled pigmentation and ridiculously small dorsal fin that is characteristic of the largest animal on the planet. Almost simultaneously,

Long-beaked Common Dolphins

a shout rang out among the researchers on the ship: "Blue Whale!" We followed the Blue Whale for several minutes as it moved away from the Fin Whales and began diving, lifting its flukes in search of a meal of its own down in the depths of the ocean. Too bad my photos of that magical day are not as sharp as my memory!

Yes, trying to determine my best day of whale-watching in the Sea of Cortez is difficult indeed. Each day in this magnificent locale holds a special place in my heart, but one day in particular stands above all the others.

It was one of those glorious days at sea that every whale-watcher dreams of. Sunny skies, warm air temperatures, and the surface of the sea was as smooth as glass. Every little ripple upon the ocean was exaggerated. You could see a flying fish leap out of the water and splash back down again from several hundred feet away with the unaided eye. I was working on a research vessel conducting line transect studies in order to ascertain population sizes of cetaceans in the region. Our work day started at first light. Right off the bat we had a large group of Long-beaked Common Dolphins leaping along the ship as the sun rose above the horizon in the background. Talk about a picture-perfect postcard. The dolphins leapt and played in the ship's quarter wake as this species often does. As the dolphins departed our vessel, we continued on our predetermined trackline.

As we started to reach deep water, I caught sight of a Dwarf Sperm Whale logging at the surface about two miles from the ship. As a general rule, these tiny whales are usually observed only on the calmest days and then only for a few seconds as they rest at the surface. This particular animal stayed at the surface for well over three minutes and allowed us wonderful looks through the binoculars from a distance of nearly a thousand feet (300 m). Brilliant! Not five minutes after our Dwarf Sperm Whale sighting we soon found ourselves in the company of two Blainville's Beaked Whales. Beaked whales are among the least-known, least-studied families of whales—not to mention mammals—in the world. Their preference for deep water and inconspicuous behavior make sightings a coup for any whale-watcher. We watched amazed as a pair of Blainville's Beaked Whales surfaced slowly just over 300 feet (100 m) off the bow of the ship. One of the whales was an adult male, evident by its two teeth above the strongly arched jawline. In the calm sea conditions, we could even see the stalk barnacles growing on the teeth.

How could it get any better than this? Here we were just two hours into the survey day and we had the privilege to see two species that are rarely, and I mean rarely, observed in the wild. As if to answer that question a shout rang out on the flying bridge: "Cuvier's Beaked Whales at 45° off the starboard bow." Sure enough, a small group of three could be seen slow rolling at the surface not far from our ship's trackline. Wow, two species of beaked whales in less than half an hour!

Little did I know at the time that we were passing through a high-density area of cetaceans that specialize in feeding on deepwater species of squid. Before the day was over we would cover over 50 miles (90 km) of ocean and document 10 species of cetaceans including my first looks at a family of five Pygmy Beaked Whales (the smallest member in the family Ziphiidae), a large group of over 30 Sperm Whales, one huge group of Risso's Dolphins, a group of Pantropical Spotted Dolphins, four more sightings of Dwarf Sperm Whales, two more sightings of *Mesoplodon* beaked whales (species unknown), and two more sightings of Cuvier's Beaked Whale. The day ended just as it had started: calm seas, clear skies, and a group of Long-beaked Common Dolphins leaping next to our ship with the sun sinking slowly below the horizon in the background. It was truly a day to remember and one that has never been repeated in all my days at sea since.

A Pelagic Trip to the Cordell Bank—a brief encounter with the denizens of the deep

Graeme Cresswell

"Hi Debbie, it's Graeme Cresswell phoning from England. I'm planning to come over to California this summer and was hoping to get some photos of Blue Whales."

"Well, you should come on our Cordell Bank trip in August. It's the best time to see Blues and the Bank is one of the most reliable places to find them."

"Really? How often do you see them?"

"Every year since '86 and we haven't missed them yet."

"Every year?"

"Yep."

"Right, count me in. I'll see you there!"

Eight months later, on a glorious August day, I was quayside in Bodega Bay, California, waiting to board the *Tracer* for the Shearwater Journeys pelagic trip to the Cordell Bank.

The Cordell Bank is a National Marine Sanctuary that covers an area of over 300 square miles (800 sq km) off the northern California coast. It is located on the continental shelf about 50 miles (80 km) northwest of San Francisco. The main feature of the sanctuary is an offshore granitic bank 5 miles (8 km) wide by 10 miles (16 km) long that rises to within 52 feet (15 m) of the ocean's surface.

Once trip leader Debbie Shearwater had done a roll call and loaded several cans of fish oil and two large bags of popcorn onto the boat, we headed slowly out of the harbor. The shorelines and mudflats around Bodega Bay were teeming with migrating shorebirds—hundreds of Marbled Godwits, Western Sandpipers and Red-necked Phalaropes were feeding feverishly, refueling before the next stage of their southward journeys to Central America. Rounding Bodega Point we entered the open waters of the Pacific Ocean and headed due

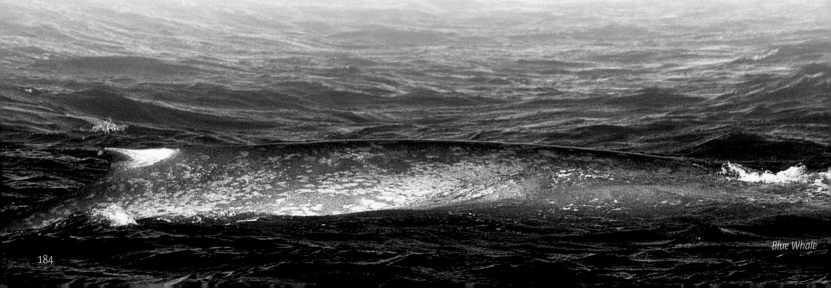

Blue Whale

west toward the Bank. The birders started dropping pieces of popcorn off the stern to ensure we had a constant stream of gulls following us, which in turn might later attract rarer seabirds into our wake.

The morning was overcast with palls of dense fog hanging over the surface. There was only a hint of a breeze and a long, rolling swell from the northwest. We were barely an hour out of port when the skipper spotted a blow several miles away on our starboard side. I scanned ahead with binoculars but could see nothing. The skipper shouted, "Two o'clock," and this time we all saw two tall spouts in the distance. In the windless conditions the whales' blows hung like tall columns of smoke before dissipating slowly in the damp air. Although the whales were still over two miles away the skipper was confident we had found a pair of Blue Whales.

As we slowly approached the position of the last blows we spotted the telltale oily flukeprints of the whales. Our boat was now idling and as several minutes passed we continually scanned in all directions. Finally, after what seemed like an eternity we heard a great exhalation several feet from our port side. I wheeled around and almost simultaneously two Blue Whales majestically rolled to the surface showing off their huge shoulders, long backs and tiny dorsal fins. As the whales surfaced again they moved even closer to the boat revealing what beautiful creatures they are; above the surface they are colored mottled gray, but through these clear oceanic waters they take on varying hues of turquoise and ultramarine. It was amazing to think that the water depth here was just 196 feet (60 m) and these 82-foot-long (25 m) animals could reach the bottom in seconds with just a flick of their tails.

We drifted forwards, slowly tracking the whales, and after another surfacing sequence the boat branched away and moved back onto our original course. It was a fantastic start to our trip and amazingly we were to encounter at least a further 10 Blue Whales throughout the day.

After two hours cruising at a steady eight knots we were within a few miles of the Bank and small numbers of shearwaters and petrels began to appear. At the stern the stream of gulls and Brown Pelicans had now been joined by small flocks of Sabine's Gulls and Parasitic Jaegers. Someone yelled out "Albatross!" and the first Black-footed Albatross of the day wheeled effortlessly across the bow. These magnificent birds are known to commute between the rich feeding grounds at the Cordell Bank and their breeding grounds on Midway Atoll, several thousand miles to the west!

As we moved across the Bank our vessel put up great rafts of Sooty Shearwaters that were keeping our bird counters fully occupied. Here we encountered a small party of Humpback Whales. These animals seemed to be feeding and one of the whales lunged three-quarters clear of the surface, scattering the massed ranks of shearwaters and petrels. Great quantities of water and small fish spilled out from its jaws with many of the seabirds picking through the leftovers. In the feeding frenzy the Humpbacks were joined by a porpoising group of California Sea Lions.

We cruised slowly back and forth through the many flocks of shearwaters looking for unusual seabirds and other cetaceans. After an hour we decided to move west again and into offshore waters where hopefully greater prizes awaited us. As we headed away from the Bank and into deep water the number of seabirds dropped dramatically. It was approaching midday, the mist had cleared completely and we were now sailing under blue skies and across glassy seas.

We continued to head west, crossing over the steep continental slope, when Debbie spotted a few blows on the horizon. Unlike the tall spouts of the Blues we had seen earlier these were much smaller, like circular puffs of white smoke. I caught a glimpse of some dark, sleek bodies rolling smoothly at the surface. These appeared to be much smaller whales and were moving in a tight formation. Through my binoculars I could make out a bulbous head and pointed snout on a couple of the animals—we had found a group of beaked whales and Debbie was pretty sure that they were Baird's. I couldn't believe my luck. I had hoped to see some beaked whales but was told it was a long shot—"a one-in-20-trip occurrence and they usually disappear long before you get near them."

As we approached to within 1,600 feet (500 m) of the pod I could clearly make out the whales' distinct beaks and melons. They were all surfacing and diving in unison, but they still remained at or near the surface and did not appear to be diving deep. The skipper slowed the boat to a virtual crawl and the whales surfaced again within 160 feet (50 m) of our starboard side, accompanied by our shrieks of delight. We counted 13 animals and they all seemed incredibly tactile, continually rubbing their bodies against one another. The whales were dark brown and heavily criss-crossed with white scars. Several animals raised their heads above the water while others breached partially clear of the surface. We stayed with them for about 20 minutes before they all dived together and were gone. We sailed slowly away from their flukeprints and headed west again, elated with our fantastic encounter with these rare denizens of the deep.

We continued into deeper waters and the skipper informed us that we were way over the "drop-off" and it was at least 8,200 feet (2,500 m) to the bottom! We were now over the abyss where many hours could pass without sighting a single bird or mammal. The teeming rafts of seabirds and whales over the Bank just 10 miles (16 km) east seemed like another world. However, this was the realm of enigmatic beaked whales, albatrosses and rare gadfly petrels.

Debbie decided to stop the boat for a late lunch and at the same time put out some fish oil to see if we could attract any unusual seabirds. Looking around the boat I was far from convinced this would work as the surrounding ocean appeared totally devoid of life—even the trail of gulls had left us behind.

In the glassy seas the oily slick drifted slowly south from the stern. Five minutes passed and nothing happened. I was just finishing lunch and giving my camera a dust down when a solitary Black-footed Albatross cruised into our wake. Two more albatrosses soon appeared while several Ashy Storm-Petrels were now fluttering over the slick. I was amazed—in less than a quarter of an hour nearly 50 seabirds had found our tiny boat—testament to the incredible sense of smell that these ocean wanderers possess.

We waited by the slick for nearly an hour and watched several species of seabirds come and go but we didn't attract any gadfly petrels that the birders were hoping for. It was now two o'clock and we were nearly 30 miles (50 km) from Bodega Head, so it was time to turn the boat around and head back.

As we neared the continental drop-off again, a small whale surfaced just a few feet from the bow and surged towards us. At the last minute the whale dived under the boat, almost to within touching distance of those observers at the bow. Most people only got a brief look at it and thought it might be a Killer Whale, but luckily I got a clear view of the animal. It appeared to be a small, predominantly gray-colored whale with a short but distinct beak. I was pretty certain that it was a small beaked whale, but I needed another look. Debbie was now on the roof of the bridge, animatedly yelling at us to get a photo of the whale when it resurfaced. Amazingly, the whale gave a virtually repeat performance, surfacing this time on the starboard side about 160 feet (50 m) away from us, and then swimming toward the bow and under the boat. This time we all got a better view and it was clearly a beaked whale of the genus *Mesoplodon*—one of the most rarely seen whales in the North American Pacific. But which species was it? We needed to get a decent look at its head, and ideally some good photographs. After an agonizing wait the whale briefly surfaced again, but it was a little farther away this time and soon vanished. Unfortunately none of the photographers managed to get a picture—believe me, we all tried!

Much discussion on the whale's identification ensued. Some of the leaders thought it might be Hubbs' Beaked Whale, others, Blainville's. However, I saw no raised jawline nor protruding teeth, although we could have easily overlooked them. It looked like one of the smaller members of its genus, so perhaps it was the recently discovered Perrin's Beaked Whale? Unfortunately we would probably never know, as without photos or a clear view of an adult male's beak, identification would prove virtually impossible.

Despite not knowing which species it was we felt extremely fortunate to have had a close encounter with such a rare animal. Little did I realize just how rare this sighting was, as Debbie later told me that in over 2,000 pelagic trips in the North Pacific she had seen *Mesoplodon* beaked whales on just two previous occasions.

As we crossed the Bank again we passed several more Humpbacks and were briefly joined by a small pod of Pacific White-sided Dolphins. We reached Bodega at about five o'clock after over 10 hours at sea. Everyone was extremely tired but elated. We had seen over a dozen Blue Whales, 20 Humpbacks, 13 Baird's Beaked Whales, one *Mesoplodon* beaked whale, 15 Pacific White-sided Dolphins, over 100 California Sea Lions and a lone Northern Fur Seal. The bird list was equally impressive and included over 20,000 Sooty Shearwaters and 60 Black-footed Albatrosses.

Since that first cruise I have been on several more trips to the Cordell Bank. All have produced many wonderful marine mammal sightings, but none has been so memorable as my first. If you get a chance to visit this very special place, don't miss the boat!

The Otters of Untamed Alaska

Heidi Pearson

Texas Agricultural and Mechanical University (Texas A&M) researchers and Earthwatch volunteers have spent many fabulous days with the Sea Otters of Alaska during recent summers. Our research site is Simpson Bay, on the eastern side of Prince William Sound, Alaska.

Simpson Bay is marked by fjords, a temperate rainforest and abundant wildlife. The scenery is absolutely breathtaking, with steep green forested mountains that are iced with snow and plunge into the ocean. I always enjoyed marveling at the shapes and patterns of the fjords during the skiff ride back to camp after a day's work. In a temperate rainforest, rain is abundant and sunshine can be in short supply. The clouds and mist do provide their own beauty, though, creating a scene of "Otters in the Mist" as the fjords take on a different mood. One learns not to take the sun for granted, and when the clouds do lift you realize that a few gray days are a small price to pay for the glorious colors that spring to life in Simpson Bay after the rain. The sun plays an especially important role at Simpson Bay's latitude of 45° north, where it never fully sets during the height of summer. The result is true "Northern Exposure."

Brown and Black Bears flourish in the forests around Simpson Bay. Seeing a bear is always a thrill, and reason for a break in the research. On our best bear-viewing day, we saw eight different Black Bears—two single animals, and two females with two cubs each. What a treat! During the early part of the summer, we regularly saw Brown Bears along the shore. However, once the salmon started running upstream to spawn, the Brown Bears followed and disappeared from our sight. Catching salmon in the shallow streams of the bay is quite an easy meal for a bear. Berries are another favorite food, and they can strip the bushes bare. Humans also enjoy picking and eating berries, and we would sometimes go to a patch only to find that the bears had beaten us to it!

Numerous bird species also abound in Simpson Bay, and the most impressive is undoubtedly the Bald Eagle. The eagle population seems to be quite healthy in this area, and they are commonly seen perched on the uppermost branches of trees or flying above the water in search of food. One breeding pair gave us a special treat by building their nest right along our skiff route from camp to the research site. At the start of the summer, we could just barely make out the eaglets' small heads popping out of the nest from time to time. By the end of the summer, we were fortunate to have the opportunity to see them take some of their first flights. It isn't easy to land on a branch! Other animals

Sea Otters

188

living in and around Simpson Bay include the Harbor Seal, Steller Sea Lion, Dall's Porpoise, Harbor Porpoise, River Otter, Coyote, and, on rare occasions, the Killer Whale.

Our primary focus, however, is the Sea Otter. Sea Otters are special animals to study for a number of reasons. They are unique among marine mammals in that they lack blubber and have a relatively small body size. In order to compensate for this and maintain the proper body temperature in cold waters, their insulating layer of fur is the densest of any animal, with as many as 164,662 hairs per square centimeter on some parts of the body. This dense fur requires a Sea Otter to spend about 15% of its day grooming to keep it clean. Additionally, they need an increased metabolic rate in order to keep warm in cold waters. This demands a great deal of energy and food, and it is estimated that Sea Otters consume 23–33% of their body weight in food each day.

Sea Otters are referred to as a keystone species, meaning they have a large impact on other species in their community by influencing species structure and relationships. Keystone species maintain balance and stability in the ecosystem, and changes in their abundance may cause a series of events affecting organisms throughout the entire food chain. In some areas, Sea Otters have been called the most important species in the coastal ecosystem because of their ability to maintain herbivore densities by feeding on various mollusk and crustacean species. The main prey of Sea Otters in many areas are sea urchins. When Sea Otter populations are stable, their predation on sea urchins limits the sea urchin's voracious appetite for grazing kelp, thereby resulting in low sea urchin densities and increased vegetation. Conversely, when Sea Otter numbers are low, sea urchin abundance increases and kelp densities decrease.

There is a healthy Sea Otter population in Simpson Bay, numbering approximately 150 animals. Sea Otters exhibit sexual segregation, meaning males and females live in areas separated by as many as 150 kilometers. Simpson Bay is a female area, consisting of females and their dependent pups. Generally, the only males present are young pups or adult males that have established breeding territories to be near the females. Juvenile males and non-territorial males inhabit a separate male area. Therefore, male–female contact usually occurs only in the context of mating. Sea Otters have a polygynous mating system, meaning a single male will mate with multiple females each year, while each female successfully mates with only one male.

Specifically, Sea Otters exhibit resource defense polygyny, meaning females are attracted to a male's territory based on the resources it contains and not necessarily the male himself. Female Sea Otters may be attracted to a territory based on a number of factors, such as prey availability, resting areas, protection from wind and waves, accessibility and total area defended from harassment by other males. Males then attempt to mate with those females that feed or rest in their territories.

One component of the project was to photograph and observe Sea Otters, and one particular morning spent doing just that remains vivid in my memory. It was our third day observing a Sea Otter mating pair, whom we named "Rhett" and "Scarlett." For the previous two days, the pair was inseparable. Rhett followed Scarlett's every move, from swimming to feeding to resting. They even dove in synchrony, like a well-rehearsed dance. Rhett's close attentiveness to Scarlett was vital. His primary goal was to mate with Scarlett, but his secondary purpose was to prevent other males from mating with her. Rhett wanted to be sure it was his genes that were going to be passed on to Scarlett's future pup.

All seemed well in "Love Cove," until the moment of the "big break-up" on the third day. Rhett and Scarlett were no longer diving in synchrony while they were feeding. While one was diving underwater, the other was feeding on the surface. This made it difficult for Rhett to keep track of Scarlett, and was the first indication that something was amiss. As we watched, we gradually saw Scarlett moving farther and farther away from Rhett while he was diving. Within a few minutes, she had moved to the opposite side of the cove. When Rhett surfaced from his last dive, Scarlett was out of his sight. He began calling and searching for her. Another female and her pup were feeding in the cove, close to Rhett. He approached the female, apparently confusing her for Scarlett. In the midst of this confusion, Scarlett quickly and quietly swam out of the cove, unnoticed by Rhett.

Sheep Bay, Prince William Sound

Rhett searched for Scarlett for nearly an hour. After leaving the female and pup, he searched the rest of the cove, swimming quickly and calling out for her. The previous day, we had observed Scarlett hauled out on a rock in the cove. Rhett briefly hauled himself up on this rock, but did not find Scarlett. Back in the water again, he continued to call for Scarlett. His calls were more like screams filled with panic and sorrow, and it really was a heart-wrenching thing for us human observers to hear. More confusion ensued as another pup in the cove answered Rhett's calls, mistaking them for those of its mother. Rhett then encountered the pup's mother and sniffed her, but he soon discovered she was not Scarlett either. He came across a third female and sniffed her, but she was still not the one he was looking for.

After thoroughly searching the cove, Rhett began patroling the rest of his territory. Being a territorial male, Rhett would normally spend several hours each day swimming along the edge of his territory, searching for females and guarding against unwanted intrusions by other males. Now, Rhett was swimming quickly along the periphery of his territory in the hope of finding Scarlett. He made a wide arc from inside the cove, outside to the bay, and back to the cove again. He made one last call for Scarlett once back in the cove, but he was still left unanswered. Finally, he stopped searching and began to feed on clams. We joked that he had given up hope of finding her again, and was consoling himself with food.

What we observed was truly a unique occurrence in the life of the Sea Otter, and one that I feel extremely fortunate to have witnessed. We never found out where Scarlett swam after her departure from Rhett, and only saw her one more time that summer. We saw Rhett many more times over the course of the summer, and watched him have many encounters with other females. However, none were as dramatic as his "affair" with Scarlett. Rhett mated several more times throughout the summer, but Scarlett most likely mated only with Rhett. Perhaps we will see Scarlett and her new pup when we go back to Simpson Bay next summer.

Heidi Pearson is a Ph.D. student in the Department of Wildlife and Fisheries Sciences at Texas A&M University. She studied the behavior of territorial male sea otters in Prince William Sound for her Master's research, and has published her findings in *Aquatic Mammals* and *Canadian Journal of Zoology*. Currently, she is studying the social behavior of dusky dolphins in New Zealand.

The Friendly Gray Whales of San Ignacio Lagoon

Rick M. Harbo

We jostle and shake for four hours as we slowly make our way out to the lagoon. My daughter, Jennifer, and I are traveling to see what the locals call the "desert whales" of Mexico. It is March and the road is wet and often divides into several tracks. Johnny, our driver, proceeds cautiously, as he knows repairs take time and parts are not readily available in this remote area of the Baja Peninsula. For over 12 years, Johnny Friday has driven this road to Campo Cortez at San Ignacio Lagoon on the Pacific Coast. He developed a friendship and eventually a partnership with a local fisherman, Maldo Ficher. Together they built a nature retreat on the remote desert lagoon and formed a whale-watching business, the Baja Adventure Company.

We stop at the side of the road for a drink and a stretch; I quickly snap off a roll of film. We're amazed at the diversity of cactuses along our journey across the Baja Peninsula. The world's tallest cactus, the Cordon Cactus, grows to 65 feet (20 m), and often dominates the landscape. Dr. Marie Dalcourt, our naturalist for the trip, advised that there were several hundred species of cactuses found in this desert region, ranging from Giant Barrel Cactus to the rambling growth of the Galloping Cactus. The Mexican Fence Post Cactus is often planted in rows to make a living fence. Mexico has more species and specimens of cactuses than any other country in the world.

Our excitement grows as a row of white canvas tents come into view. They are situated on a low bank at the edge of the water. This will be our base camp for the next few days as we journey out into the lagoon to view the Gray Whales. San Ignacio Lagoon, a wildlife reserve since 1979, was recently threatened by a proposed development of a saltworks by the Mexican government and the Mitsubishi Corporation. International pressure caused the government to withdraw its support and maintain this undisturbed wildlife refuge. The lagoon is one of the few undeveloped breeding grounds for Gray Whales, a haven before they make their long annual migration north to the Bering Sea to feed. This 6,200-mile (10,000-km) trip is the longest migration of any mammal, and we hope we are going to be fortunate to rub and scratch one of these giants.

Gray Whale

Jennifer and I have often witnessed the Gray Whales in the spring as they quickly passed by Vancouver Island on the way north. There is an active whale-watching industry on the west coast of Vancouver Island that views Gray Whales, 35 to 50, that do not migrate any farther north than Vancouver Island. They spend the spring and summer feeding on herring spawn, then a variety of planktonic animals in the water column. The Gray Whale is the only whale known to feed on the bottom, rolling on its side and scooping up a mouthful of sand and mud. Dr. Jim Darling and underwater photographer Flip Nicklin confirmed that the massive tongue acts a plunger, first to vacuum up the sediment and then to force the water and mud out through the baleen plates to screen out a meal of small crustaceans (shrimp and crab-like creatures).

A margarita, a wonderful dinner in the palapa dining hut and we are off to our tent for the night. Inside the tent, two cots sit on the sand with a runner of carpet between them. Johnny reminded Jen and me to shake our shoes in the morning, a precaution to avoid the wrath of the local scorpions. I lay on my cot, cold in my sleeping bag, listening to the bark of coyotes. Marie convinced Jennifer and I that the coyotes were small and not at all aggressive. Later, as I trek to the outhouse, their eyes shine in the light of my flashlight and they quickly disappear into the cloak of darkness.

When the lagoon is calm, the powerful blows of the whales often interrupt the quiet. Not tonight! The wind begins to whip our tent and I stumble out in the night to tie down any loose bits of tent that I can. I shiver as I crawl back into my down bag, remembering the brochure referred to this as "safari style ambience."

It sounds like another fishing story, but Cummings and Mallan's *Mexican Handbook* recounts how the coyotes in Baja occasionally fish for crabs: "The coyote's furry tail is placed in the water, waiting for a crab to grab on. Then, with a flick of the tail, the crab is tossed ashore. Before the crab can recover from the shock, the coyote is busy enjoying a fine crab feast."

I wake to an orange light bursting through the walls of the canvas. I open the front flap of the tent and watch the sun rise over the lagoon from my cot. A variety of shore birds walk along the beach, feeding on the banquet exposed on the mudflats by the low tide. I recognize Brant Geese, a reminder of home. The Brant Wildlife Festival at Parksville, on the east coast of Vancouver Island, celebrates the annual return of these geese each spring, where they feed on the rich shores.

Immediately after breakfast, Jen, Zack, Marie and I join our whale-watching guide, Maldo, and walk out to the small point. This is Zack's first trip also. A kayaker from New England, he jumped at the offer of a job as nature guide and kayak leader at the camp. A small fibreglass boat, or panga, is anchored just off a rocky outcrop and Maldo hauls the rope and brings the panga to shore. We board and set off with great anticipation.

Maldo's face breaks into a grin as we round the point and a Gray Whale breaches in the distance. "Watch," he says, "they always breach three times in a row. One time, a whale breached eight times!" Sure enough, twice more the whale rises out of the water, turns and lands with a great splash.

Maldo stands at the stern of the boat and holds the steering arm and controls of the motor. He slows the panga as we approach a large mother, almost 46 feet (14 m) long, and her calf. "Splash water at them," Marie cries, "she will bring her baby." Soon the large mother and her calf slowly approach the boat. A gentle lifting of the boat as the whale rubs up and under the boat makes us a little nervous, all except for Maldo. "I haven't had anyone land in the water yet," he says with a reassuring smile.

The mother raises her large head at the side of the boat and patiently rests as we rub and scratch her back. It is for good reason that the only boats allowed in the lagoon are those guided by the local fishermen.

Marie cautions, "Do not touch the eye, blowholes or fins of the whales. This will disturb them." The mother constantly swims immediately below her calf, and gently moves the calf towards the boat for a greeting. A burst of bubbles rises to the surface. We are not sure if this behavior, called bubble blasting, is a greeting or a sign of aggression. The head of the calf rises out of the water to expose a large eye, shutters click and there are cries of excitement. I shoot many frames and capture Jen and Zack's first time rubbing and scratching the back of the calf. I wonder what other wild animal would bring its young to humans for contact?

How different this is from the aggression of the mother whales and the harrowing experiences of whalers in earlier times on these breeding grounds that caused them to call these whales "hard-head" and "devil-fish." According to Charles Scammon, the 19th-century whaler, "hard-head" arose from the fact that the animals have a great propensity to root boats when coming in contact with them, in the same manner that hogs upset their empty troughs. He chronicled the cruel practice of harpooning calves first in order to draw the mothers within "darting distance." The enraged mother would chase the boats and overturn them with her head or "dash them in pieces with a stroke of her ponderous flukes."

On this day, we do not feel threatened at all by these giants. We look into the clear water and see that the mother's head and body is decorated with clusters of barnacles, a species that grows exclusively on these whales. What seemed at first to be pink patches, were at closer examination small crab-like crustaceans known as whale lice. Gray Whales are known to be the most encrusted of all the whales. We slowly move off as another panga approaches and it is their turn to interact with the whales. Maldo tells us, "We take turns counting the whales each week as they arrive in December. By the end of March there may be as many as 300 whales in the lagoon."

As we race to the outer reaches of the lagoon, suddenly a small group of Common Bottlenose Dolphins joins us to bow ride and then just as quickly

departs. Brown Pelicans bob up and down on the waves. Soon, the telltale heart-shaped blows of the Gray Whales lead us to another group. One spyhops, gently rising straight out of the water to get a better look at the visitors. We move to investigate a group of whales on the surface creating a great deal of splashing. "This appears to be mating behavior," says Maldo. "Mating usually involves several whales, but it is surprising to see a female with a calf engaged in mating." Marie informs us that the gestation period is 12 to 13 months and a female will have a calf every other year.

Then Maldo announces it is time to return to the camp for lunch. We groan to be leaving, but our spirits are high as the boat heads toward camp. Jen and I smile at each other and we realize we have had an unforgettable experience with the friendly Gray Whales of San Ignacio Lagoon.

Rick M. Harbo, B.Sc., author of *Whelks to Whales—A Field Guide to Marine Life of Alaska, British Columbia, Washington and Oregon; Tidepool and Reef; The Edible Seashore; Guide to Western Seashore*, and *Shells and Shellfish of the Pacific Northwest*, is one of the leading marine writers and photographers in his field. He is a marine biologist with Fisheries and Oceans Canada in Nanaimo, BC, where he lives with his wife and children.

Marine Mammal Conservation in the North American Pacific

Our perceptions of marine mammals have changed greatly in the last hundred years. Once looked upon entirely for their commercial uses, marine mammals now enjoy complete protection in the North American Pacific under the Marine Mammal Protection Act. The history of marine mammals in this region is as varied as it is long.

Marine mammals have the unfortunate distinction of being one of the most relentlessly exploited groups of animals on the planet. For centuries, humans have hunted cetaceans, pinnipeds and Sea Otters for their oil, meat and fur.

Shore-based whaling stations along the North American Pacific were prevalent during the 1800s and early 1900s. Many species of cetaceans were targeted, and several were hunted in order to produce a diverse range of products including soap, shampoo, candles, machine lubricants, and even glycerine for explosives. Whaling stations operated throughout the North American Pacific until stocks of whales were hunted so heavily that populations crashed and commercial whaling was no longer a lucrative business. Some whaling stations endured late into the 1900s, targeting species of lesser commercial value such as Baird's Beaked Whales and Killer Whales. A whaling station operated in San Francisco Bay until 1971 when it was shut down by the US Department of Commerce. In that year commercial whaling was banned to all US vessels.

Since that time, some species of whales have shown a remarkable recovery in their population sizes. The increase in the population of North American Gray Whales represents the most successful recovery of any large species of whale. Due to heavy hunting, Gray Whales were once considered close to extinction in the eastern North Pacific. However, in the last 50 years, Gray Whale numbers have increased so much that the species was taken out of the Endangered Species Act in 1994. The current population estimates for this species place them at or greater than those of the pre-whaling era. Current population estimates for Blue, Fin and Humpback Whales in the North American Pacific suggest that they are also recovering from the onslaught of the industrial whaling era. It is estimated that over 3,000 Blue Whales, 14,000 Fin Whales and 6,000 Humpback Whales now inhabit the North Pacific. While these numbers are but a fraction of what the population sizes were before the advent of whaling, it is nonetheless encouraging to see these stocks increasing in size. It should be noted that one species of large whale in this region is not increasing in population size—the North Pacific Right Whale. The total population, which probably numbers in the tens of animals, will likely become extinct in the near future. Exactly why the numbers of this species of whale are decreasing while other species' populations are increasing in this region is not entirely known.

Commercial exploitation also decimated many pinniped populations in the North American Pacific, with some species nearing extinction before hunting was banned or became economically unviable. Due to a combination of aboriginal hunting and commercial exploitation, Northern Elephant Seals were considered to be extinct by the late 1800s. When an isolated population was discovered in the late 1880s on Guadalupe Island, seven of the eight seals were shot by a scientific expedition requiring specimens because the species remained poorly described! Again Northern Elephant Seals were effectively extinct but a small population did survive and steadily increased in size and range throughout the 20th century. The Guadalupe Fur Seal endured a similar fate. Following extensive hunting throughout the 19th century, it was considered to be extinct by the 1920s. It wasn't until 1954 that 14 individuals were discovered on Guadalupe Island. Like the Northern Elephant Seal, its population has shown a steady recovery, but the rate of recovery has been much slower. Currently the breeding population is restricted to just two islands, and its status is classified as threatened and depleted.

With a supreme pelage containing the greatest density of fur of any mammal, it is no wonder that the Sea Otter was sought after by Native people and commercial operators alike. When otter pelts finally found their way onto European and Asian markets, the Sea Otter was hunted almost to extinction. From 1741 to 1911, almost one million Sea Otters were killed before the hunting was finally stopped. Since then, the population of this species has rebounded strongly.

Though many populations of marine mammal in the North American Pacific have increased following over-exploitation in the past, some have also recently shown worrying declines and it is clear that they still face many threats. The Steller Sea Lion population has dropped by approximately 80% since the 1970s. The precise cause of this decline is unclear, but there is some evidence to suggest that their prey species have declined, perhaps due to a combination of commercial fishing and climatic shifts.

Probably the most prevalent threats to marine mammals in this region are increasing fishing pressure, bycatch in various fishing gear, pollution and climate change. As the human population increases, the greater affect it has on the environment. Increased fishing affects Killer Whale populations in Vancouver and Puget Sound by decreasing the number of prey items available to the whales. Gillnets and drift nets in the region are indiscriminate in what they catch—and countless numbers of cetaceans, pinnipeds and Sea Otters have died over the years. However, pollution is probably the greatest threat to marine mammals in the region today. Humans dump tons of industrial waste, agricultural chemicals, untreated sewage, plastics and radioactive discharges into the ocean every day. These toxins remain in the environment for many years. Marine mammals, being at the top of the food chain, accumulate toxins in their tissues over a period of time, which in turn hampers their immune system. Recent tissue samples gathered from Killer Whales in Puget Sound and Monterey Bay show that they are among the most polluted animals on Earth. Under today's standards, these whales could legally be considered toxic waste.

With the bad also comes the good. Whale-watching in this region has raised the public's awareness of the plight of cetaceans in the North American Pacific. Whale-watching is a multimillion-dollar-a-year industry, with operations being found from Alaska to Baja California. People spend their hard-earned money just to experience the majesty and beauty of whales and dolphins in their natural environment. Among the highlights that can be observed in this region with ease are: Humpback Whales lunge feeding in Frederick Sound, Southeast Alaska; Killer Whales in Puget Sound, Washington; Blue Whales during the fall in Monterey Bay, California; and Gray Whales in the breeding lagoons of Baja California. Whale-watching continues to grow within the North American Pacific and has introduced millions of people to these magnificent animals. As a direct result, more people are giving money to conservation organizations that strive to protect marine mammals and the environment in which they live.

No longer viewed as animals to be killed for profit, marine mammals are now perceived by the public as magnificent animals that deserve special attention. As greater pressures are placed upon the environment in the coming years, let us hope that this perception remains so that future generations can be thrilled by the sight of a Humpback Whale breaching on the open ocean, a group of Pacific White-sided Dolphins playing in the wake of a passing ship, or a raft of Sea Otters wrapped in the kelp. These are marvels of the natural world that need to be protected and enjoyed for generations to come.

AMERICAN CETACEAN SOCIETY
Since 1967

www.ACSonline.org

As ethical publishers, **WILD**Guides and Harbour Publishing will donate a percentage of the profits of each book sold to the American Cetacean Society (ACS). As the oldest whale conservation group in the world, ACS protects whales, dolphins, porpoises and their habitats through public education, research grants, and conservation actions. For more information on the ACS please visit their website at: http://www.acsonline.org/.

MISSION STATEMENT

The American Cetacean Society is dedicated to the protection of whales, dolphins, and porpoises, and their habitats, through education and outreach, conservation advocacy, and facilitating research.

The American Cetacean Society (ACS) is the oldest whale conservation group in the world. Founded in 1967, it is a non-profit, volunteer membership organization with regional US chapters and members in 22 countries. Our National Headquarters is in San Pedro, California.

Chapters are located in Puget Sound, Washington; San Francisco, California; Monterey, California; Channel Islands, California; Los Angeles, California; and Orange County, California.

ACS works to protect whales, dolphins, porpoises, and their habitats through education, conservation and research.

We believe the best way to protect cetaceans is by educating the public about these remarkable animals and the problems they face in their increasingly threatened habitats.

ACS seeks to educate through its publications and the development of teaching aids. Cetacean curriculum and whale, dolphin & porpoise fact sheets are available on our website. Educational material may also be mail ordered. ACS also publishes a journal, *Whalewatcher*. Some ACS Chapters offer grants to support cetacean research by biologists and graduate students.

Glossary

Abyssal plain: The ocean floor beyond the continental shelf.

Acoustics: The study of sound.

Aggregation: When several individuals or groups of a particular species of cetacean come together in order to hunt, mate, raise young or defend themselves against predators.

Anterior: Toward the front of the body.

Atoll: A ring-shaped coral reef or string of coral islands, usually enclosing a shallow lagoon.

Balaenidae: The cetacean family comprising three species of Right Whale and the Bowhead Whale. They are large and bulky with a strongly arched rostrum, which in profile forms a deeply curved jawline.

Balaenopteridae: The cetacean family, also known as the "rorquals," comprising large to very large baleen whales which possess a series of throat grooves that extend underneath the lower jaw. They feed by opening their cavernous jaws as they swim along and expanding their throat grooves, vastly increasing the volume of water held within their mouths.

Baleen: Comb-like plates that grow from the upper jaw of some large whales. They are used to filter food from sea water.

Barnacle: Small, hard-shelled marine crustaceans of the subclass Cirrepedia. In the adult stages some species cling to the bodies of marine mammals.

Beach rubbing: The act of rubbing the body against a hard object such as a boulder or the sea floor. Killer Whales regularly engage in this behavior close to shore in British Columbia. Beach rubbing may help to rid unwanted parasites from the skin.

Beak: The snout, or forward-projecting jaws of a cetacean.

Beaked whale: A member of the toothed whale family Ziphiidae, all of which show a forward-projecting jaw.

Belly up: A term for lying motionless in the water with the belly pointing skyward. This often occurs during bouts of social behavior and is also employed by female whales as they attempt to avoid the attentions of males wishing to mate.

Blackfish: A colloquial term originally used by whalers to describe the predominantly black members of the family Delphinidae.

Blow: The breath of a cetacean, in which moisture-laden air is expelled from the lungs as a visible spout of water.

Blowhole(s): The nostril(s) of a cetacean.

Blubber: The layer of insulating fat below the skin of marine mammals.

Bow riding: Swimming in the pressure wave created ahead of moving vessels or large whales.

Breaching: The act of propelling the body upwards until most or all of it is clear of the water.

Bubble netting: A cooperative method employed by some species of cetacean and pinniped to catch large schools of fish or invertebrates by trapping them inside walls, columns or clouds of bubbles created by releasing air under water.

Bull: The adult male of a large animal, such as an elephant, pinniped or whale.

Bycatch: The proportion of a catch that is not made up of the targeted species, and is therefore caught incidentally.

Calf: Young marine mammal still being nursed by its mother.

Callosity: Rough, lumpy patches of skin on the head of a Right Whale.

Cape: Dark region on the upper back of some cetaceans.

Carnivora: The order Carnivora consists of mammals with jaws and teeth adapted for eating flesh. Examples include pinnipeds and otters.

Cetacean: A marine mammal of the order Cetacea, which includes all the whales, dolphins and porpoises.

Chevron: A pale marking, shaped like the letter V, on the back of some Fin Whales and Pygmy Beaked Whales.

Chorus line: The coordinated movement of a group of marine mammals as they surface in a line abreast. This behavior is frequently observed in members of the blackfish family and the Risso's Dolphin, often when searching for prey.

Continental shelf: A horizontal ledge under shallow water between a continental landmass and the ocean floor.

Continental slope: A region of incline between the continental shelf and the abyssal plain.

Copepods: Tiny shrimp-like crustaceans, which form the prey of some baleen whales.

Cosmopolitan: A widely distributed animal or plant occurring in many parts of the world.

Crustacean: From the class Crustacea, crustaceans have a hard shell and are usually aquatic. They include shrimps, crabs and lobsters.

Deep dive: A long dive. In the case of cetaceans, this often follows a succession of shorter dives which make up a surfacing sequence. In some of the larger whales, a deep dive is characterized by throwing the tail flukes high into the air.

Delphinidae: The toothed whale family, which includes all oceanic dolphins.

Depth contour: A line drawn on a sea chart connecting points of equal depth.

Diagnostic: A characteristic or set of characteristics that confirm identification.

Diurnal: During the day.

DNA: Acronym for deoxyribonucleic acid. DNA molecules carry the genetic information necessary for the function of most living cells and control the inheritance of characteristics.

Dolphin: Small cetacean that usually has a beak, conical-shaped teeth and a falcate dorsal fin.

Dorsal: A directional term meaning toward the back or upper-side.

Dorsal fin: The upper or top fin in marine vertebrates.

Drift net: A type of gillnet that is suspended in the water vertically like a curtain.

Ear flaps: External ears.

Eared seals: See Otariidae.

Echelon feeding: The coordinated movement of a group of whales as they feed side by side with jaws wide open.

Echolocation: The location of objects by reflected sound.

Ecosystem: A biological community of living organisms interacting with each other and their environment.

El Niño: A cyclical event that occurs in the eastern Pacific every few years, in which ocean currents slow, water temperatures increase and upwellings decline, often resulting in a shift in the distributions of marine mammals due to reduced food supplies.

Endangered Species Act: This law, passed in 1973 by the United States Congress, seeks to protect all wildlife in danger of extinction. The endangered species listed in the Act includes a number of marine mammals.

Endemic: Only found in a certain region.

Escarpment: A long, steep slope at the edge of a plateau (shelf).

Eschrichtiidae: A cetacean family that includes just one species, the Gray Whale.

Exoskeleton: A tough, structural body covering made of chitin. Found principally in arthropods.

Falcate: Sickle-shaped and curved backward.

Fast travel: The directional movement of a marine mammal traveling rapidly while raising only the upperparts of its body as it surfaces.

Filter feeding: A hunting technique employed by baleen whales, in which solid items such as fish or plankton are sieved by the baleen plates, which remove water from the mouth and leave a strained mass of food on the tongue.

Fish whacking: The tail of a cetacean is a powerful weapon that is sometimes used for hunting. Common Bottlenose Dolphins sometimes whack fish into the air and Killer Whales are capable of lifting porpoises and pinnipeds out of the water with a sweep of their tail flukes.

Flank: The side of the body.

Flipper: The fore limbs of marine mammals, including cetaceans, pinnipeds and manatees.

Flipper slapping: The raising of a flipper into the air before bringing it crashing down on the water's surface.

Flipper waving: Some whales, particularly the Humpback Whale, can wave one or both flippers in the air from side to side while lying on its side or back.

Flukes: The horizontally flattened tail of cetaceans, which functions as an organ of propulsion.

Fluke print: A patch of calm water that remains on the surface after a whale dives.

Food chain: The transfer of energy from green plants through a series of organisms, each being consumed by an organism from higher up the chain.

Forage: The act of looking or searching for food.

Fore flippers: The front flippers of a pinniped.

Furrier: Someone who makes or sells furs.

Gadfly petrel: Gadfly petrels form one of the largest groups of tubenosed birds, with about 30 species in the genus *Pterodroma*. The name "gadfly" refers to the petrels' pronounced stooping maneuvers in flight.

Genetics: The study of inherited characteristics.

Genus: A grouping of one or several species with distinctive characteristics, which constitute a taxonomic family.

Gestation: The period between conception and birth, during which a female is pregnant.

Gillnet: An anchored net that is suspended vertically to trap fish (and other marine life) as they swim into it, becoming entangled by their gills.

Global Positioning System (GPS): Electronic device capable of pinpointing its location on the Earth's surface based on information received from satellites.

Gregarious: Living in communities; enjoying the company of others.

Guard hairs: Long, tough and flattened hairs that protect the underfur of a mammal.

Gular pleats: See ventral pleats.

Habitat: The natural home of a species or a distinct living community.

Harem: A group of breeding females within a territory controlled by a single male.

Hauling out: The act of leaving the water at a suitable location in order to rest or molt. Such a location is known as a "haulout." Pinnipeds haul out together to breed, rest, avoid predators, molt and warm themselves.

Head slapping: A behavior sometimes seen in large whales, when the head is raised clear of the water and then slapped down rapidly on the surface.

Hind flippers: The rear flippers of a pinniped.

Hourglass pattern: Criss-cross pattern reminiscent of an hourglass in shape.

Jugging: The appearance of sea lions or fur seals resting at the surface with both hind flippers and one fore flipper exposed to conserve heat. Their bodies are held in a position reminiscent of a jug handle.

Juvenile: Young animal that is independent of its mother, but is not fully mature.

Keel: A bulge on the underside of the tail stock of some cetaceans that resembles a ship's keel.

Kelp: Typically of the genus *Laminaria*, which includes several large broad-fronded brown seaweeds that dominate nearshore habitats throughout much of the North American Pacific.

Keratin: Stiff, fibrous substance that hairs, fingernails and baleen are made of.

Keystone species: A species of which the presence or absence can be used to assess the extent to which a habitat is being exploited.

Kogidae: A family within the toothed cetaceans, consisting of two species of Sperm Whale: the Pygmy Sperm Whale and the Dwarf Sperm Whale.

Krill: Small, shrimp-like crustaceans.

Lanugo: A covering of downy hair which, in pinniped pups, is retained for a short period after birth.

Lobtailing: The act of a large whale lifting its tail high out of the water before slapping the flukes against the surface.

Logging: The habit of cetaceans resting motionless at the water's surface in a horizontal position.

Lunge feeding: The explosive movement of a whale as it rises clear of the water with its jaws wide open to catch large schools of fish or invertebrates. When executing this maneuver the whale's head and body is thrust vertically upward into the air.

Mane: Long, thick hair growing in a line along the neck of a mammal. Present in most species of eared seals.

Marine Mammal Protection Act: A law to manage and conserve marine mammals set up by the United States government in 1972.

Mass stranding: Groups of cetaceans, which may involve up to several hundred individuals, cast ashore either alive or dead in a single event.

Median ridge: A raised line on the top of the head of all rorqual whales, running between the blowholes and the tip of the rostrum.

Melon: The bulbous forehead of some toothed cetaceans.

Mesoplodon: The scientific name for a genus of the beaked whales.

Mollusk: Any species from the phylum Mollusca; soft-bodied organisms with a hard shell, such as cuttlefish, oysters and mussels.

Molt: The process of renewing a coat or plumage; hair or feathers are shed and regrown.

Morphology: The shape and form of an organism.

Mustelidae: A family within the order Carnivora, which includes otters, stoats, weasels and badgers.

Muzzle: The forward-projecting part of the face of some animals, including the mouth and nose.

Mysticeti: The order of baleen whales.

Nearshore: At sea close to shore.

North American Pacific: A region of the North Pacific which extends from southeastern Alaska south to the tip of Baja California, and includes the Gulf of California.

Oceanography: The study of the oceans.

Odontoceti: The order of toothed cetaceans.

Offshore: At sea far from shore.

Orca: Alternate name for the Killer Whale.

Otariidae: The family of eared seals of the order Carnivora, which includes fur seals and sea lions.

Panga: A small, flat-bottomed boat.

Pectoral fin / flipper: The flippers or forelimbs of a cetacean.

Pelage: The fur coat covering a mammal.

Pelagic: Oceanic, inhabiting the open sea; living in the surface waters or middle depths of the ocean.

Pelt: The skin of a fur-bearing animal, such as a Sea Otter, when it has been removed from the carcass.

Phocidae: The family of true or earless seals, belonging to the order Carnivora. These include the Harbor Seal and the Northern Elephant Seal.

Phocoenidae: The scientific name for the porpoises, the family that includes the smallest members of the toothed cetaceans.

Photoidentification: The study of animals through the passive technique of taking photographs to capture and recapture individually recognizable features.

Physeteridae: The family of toothed cetaceans, which includes only the Sperm Whale, the largest of the toothed whales.

Phytoplankton: Free-floating plants.

Plankton: Tiny, free-floating organisms drifting with the currents, including animals and plants.

Plate tectonics: Structural changes in the plates that make up the Earth's crust.

Pinniped: A term for three families within the order Carnivora: the true seals, sea lions and fur seals, and the walrus.

Pod: A discrete, coordinated group of cetaceans.

Polar: High-latitude region near a pole and characterized by a cold climate.

Porpoise: Common name for species in the toothed whale family Phocoenidae. Porpoises are small cetaceans with an indistinct beak and spade-shaped teeth.

Porpoising: Very fast movement involving arc-shaped leaps clear of the water with a clean, head-first re-entry. This behavior is generally restricted to some dolphin and pinniped species.

Posterior: Toward the back of the body.

Prey herding: The coordinated movement of a group of marine mammals as they take advantage of the instinctive schooling behavior of their prey. Individuals herd the prey in an encircling maneuver, often forcing them to the surface before attacking them.

Proboscis: A flexible, elongated snout.

Pup: A young pinniped or sea otter.

Purse-seine net: These nets capture fish that shoal by surrounding them with a deep curtain of netting. Small lead weights on the underside of the curtain ensure that the lead line sinks quickly and the net is then pursed under the shoal.

Race: Having distinct characteristics from others of the same species.

Rafting: When marine mammals, particularly Sea Otters and pinnipeds, are resting motionless at the water's surface.

Range: The area over which a species is distributed.

Reproductive cycle: The processes between one act of reproduction and the next, in which resources are invested in the next generation.

Resident: Present in the same location throughout the year.

Roll over: The rotation of the body through 360° returning to an upright position.

Rookery: A coastal location used by colonies of pinnipeds to mate, give birth and rear their young.

Rooster tail: The spray of water shaped like a rooster's tail, which occurs when some robust cetaceans move rapidly at the surface without raising their bodies clear of the water. Rooster tails are a specialty of the Dall's Porpoise.

Rorqual: A baleen whale of the family Balaenopteridae.

Rostrum: The snout of a baleen whale.

Rubbing: Marine mammals often rub against objects such as boulders, seaweed or the sides of whale-watching boats. Rubbing may help to scrape off unwanted parasites.

Running: See porpoising.

Saddle: A saddle-shaped mark that straddles the back just behind the dorsal fin in several Delphinids.

Sagittal crest: Raised forehead, which appears like a bump on top of the head in some sea lions and fur seals.

School: A shoal of fish or cetaceans moving together in a coordinated manner.

Seal: Marine mammal of the family Phocidae, Otariidae or Odobenidae, with flippers and webbed feet.

Sealice: Small crab-like crustaceans that feed on the skin of other marine creatures, including cetaceans.

Seamount: Submarine mountains that rise from the sea floor.

Sharking: Swimming just beneath the surface so that only the dorsal fin shows.

Shelf waters: Waters over the continental shelf.

Sickle-shaped: Shaped like the crescent moon.

Skim feeding: Several baleen whales regularly skim the surface with their mouths wide open to catch prey.

Skimming: Swimming at high speed with the head and chin above the surface of the water. This peculiar behavior is unique to Rough-toothed Dolphins.

Slow travel: The directional movement of a marine mammal traveling steadily while only raising the upper parts of its body as it surfaces.

Somersault: An acrobatic movement, a trademark of several dolphin species, involving the animal turning head over tail while clear of the water.

Sonar: A system for the detection of objects under water by emitting a sound and processing the information received from its reflection.

Spermaceti: A semi-liquid waxy oil that fills the spermaceti organ in the enlarged head of all Sperm Whales.

Spinning: A behavior involving the rotation of the body along the longitudinal axis during a breach. This is a specialty of the Spinner Dolphin, which may make as many as seven complete spins during a single leap.

Splashguard: Raised area in front of the blowholes of some large whales, which helps to stop water entering the blowholes during surfacing.

Spouting: See blowing.

Stranding: The process by which a marine mammal is cast ashore in a helpless state or dead.

Subadult: An individual that is no longer dependent upon its parents, but has yet to reach physical or sexual maturity.

Submarine canyon: A deep, V-shaped channel that cuts into the continental slope.

Subpolar: See subarctic.

Subtropical: A low latitude region bordering on the tropics.

Superpod: See aggregation.

Surfacing sequence: Rising to the surface several times in quick succession between deep or prolonged dives.

Spyhopping: Raising the head vertically out of the water high enough for the eyes to view above the surface. The head usually then sinks below without making a splash.

Surf riding: Like surfers, dolphins and some whales enjoy riding the lee slopes of oceanic waves or the tops of breaking waves in the surf.

Tail slapping: Small cetaceans, particularly dolphins, are capable of lifting their tail flukes above the water and bringing them crashing down. This behavior may be repeated many times in a single session.

Tail stand: This behavior involves lying vertically head down under the surface before raising the tail upward until clear of the water. Risso's Dolphins are capable of holding their flukes in this manner for up to two minutes.

Tail stock: The tapered rear part of the body from behind the dorsal fin to the tail flukes.

Tail-throwing: Flinging the flukes and tail stock sideways out of the water.

Tail-walking: During tail-walking a cetacean gives the impression that it is walking on water by holding its body in a vertical position before crashing down. This behavior is regularly observed in the Northern Right Whale Dolphin.

Temperate region: Mid-latitude region, between subarctic and subtropical waters, characterized by a mild climate.

Terminal dive: See deep dive.

Thermoregulation: A means of temperature control.

Throat grooves: Area along the throat that can be enlarged to increase the size of the mouth.

Tool usage: The constructive use of an implement. Recorded frequently in Sea Otters and occasionally in some dolphins.

Transient: A temporary visitor; used to describe non-resident Killer Whales.

Trawl: A wide-mouthed fishing net dragged behind a boat.

Tropical: Of the tropics. The region centered around the equator and between the tropics of Cancer and Capricorn. Sea surface temperatures are very warm and never drop to freezing.

Tubercles: Rounded swellings on the heads of Humpback Whales.

Tusk: Pointed tooth that protrudes from a closed mouth.

Underfur: The thick, soft under-layer of fur lying beneath the longer and coarser hair (guard hair) found in some mammals.

Ungulate: Hoofed, herbivorous mammals such as cattle and deer.

Upwelling: A water current bringing cold, nutrient-loaded water to the surface from a lower depth, thereby providing for an abundance of marine life.

Vagrant: An animal that has wandered away from its usual home.

Ventral: The lower surface.

Ventral pleats: Folded skin along the throat of all rorqual whales, which expands like a balloon to take in additional water during feeding.

Wake riding: Some species of dolphins, including Striped and Pacific White-sided Dolphins, often show a preference for riding on waves created in the wake of a vessel.

Whale: A large marine mammal of the order Cetacea, which breathes through a blowhole in the top of the head and possesses a horizontal tail.

Ziphiidae: Members of the toothed whale family known as the beaked whales.

Zooplankton: Minute animals living near the surface of the sea (the animal component of plankton).

Useful websites

Alaska / British Columbia Whale Foundation
www.sfu.ca/biology/berg/whale/abcwhale.html

American Cetacean Society **www.acsonline.org**

Baja Whales **www.netconnection.com/bajawhales.html**

Breathtaking Whales **www.breathtakingwhales.com**

Canadian Parks and Wilderness Society **www.cpawsbc.org**

Cetacean Society International **www.csiwhalesalive.org/**

Channel Islands National Marine Sanctuary **www.cinms.nos.noaa.gov/**

CoastalBC.com **www.coastalbc.com/whales/**

Coastal Ecosystems Research Foundation **www.cerf.bc.ca/index.asp**

Cordell Bank National Marine Sanctuary **www.cordellbank.noaa.gov/**

Dana Point Festival of Whales **www.dpfestivalofwhales.com/**

Earthwatch Institute **www.earthwatch.org**

Greenpeace **www.greenpeace.org**

Gulf of the Farallones National Marine Sanctuary **www.gfnms.nos.noaa.gov/**

International Fund for Animal Welfare **www.ifaw.org**

International Wildlife Coalition **www.iwc.org/**

Johnstone Strait Killer Whale Interpretive Centre Society
www.killerwhalecentre.org/

Monterey Bay Marine Sanctuary **www.mbnms.nos.noaa.gov/**

National Oceanic and Atmospheric Administration Whale Museum
www.oceanservice.noaa.gov/

Oceanographic Environmental Research Society **www.oers.ca**

Oceanic Society **www.oceanic-society.org/**

OrcaLab **www.orcalab.org/**

Orca Network **www.orcanetwork.org**

Organisation Cetacea Beaked Whale Resource **www.beakedwhaleresource.com**

Pacific Cetacean Group **www.pacificcetaceangroup.org/**

Pacific Rim Whale Festival **www.pacificrimwhalefestival.org**

Vancouver Aquarium Marine Science Centre **www.vanaqua.org/mmrr**

Whale and Dolphin Conservation Society **www.wdcs.org**

Whale Museum **www.whale-museum.org/**

Whale-Watching-Web **www.physics.helsinki.fi/whale**

WILDGuides **www.wildguides.co.uk**

Suggested further reading

Blue Whales. J. Calambokidis & J. Steiger. 1997. Colin Baxter. World Wildlife Library, UK.

Elephant Seals: Population Ecology, Behavior, and Physiology. B.J. Le Beouf & R.M. Laws. 1994. University of California Press, Berkeley, USA.

Encyclopedia of Marine Mammals. W.F. Perrin, B. Würsig & J.M. Thewissen (Eds.). 2002. Academic Press, USA.

Eye of the Whale. D. Russell. 2001. Simon & Shuster, New York.

Eyewitness Handbook of Whales, Dolphins and Porpoises. M. Carwardine. 1995. Dorling Kindersley, London.

Field Guide to the Gray Whale. B. Bennett. 1989. Sasquatch Field Guide Series, USA.

Field Guide to the Humpback Whale. M. Morris & H.J. Bernard. 1993. Oceanic Society Expeditions & Earthtrust. Sasquatch Field Guide Series, USA.

Field Guide to the Orca. C. Flaherty & D.G. Gordon. 1990. American Cetacean Society. Sasquatch Field Guide Series, USA.

Gray Whales. J. Darling. 1999. Colin Baxter. World Wildlife Library, UK.

Guide to Marine Mammals of Alaska. K. Wynne & P.A. Folkens. 2000. University of Alaska Sea Grant College Program, USA.

Guide to Marine Mammals of the World. P.A. Folkens, R.R. Reeves, B.S. Stewart, P.J. Clapham & J.A. Powell. 2002. Chanticleer Press, New York.

Killer Whales. R.W. Baird. 2002. Colin Baxter. World Wildlife Library, UK.

Killer Whales. S. Heimlich-Boran & J. Heimlich-Boran. 1994. Colin Baxter. World Wildlife Library, UK.

Porpoises. A. Read. 1999. Colin Baxter. World Wildlife Library, UK.

Sea Otters. G. Van Blaricom. 2001. Colin Baxter. World Wildlife Library, UK.

Seals and Sea Lions. D. Miller. 1998. Colin Baxter. World Wildlife Library, UK.

Seals of the World. J.E. King. 1983. Oxford University Press, Oxford.

Sperm Whales. J. Gordon. 1998. Colin Baxter. World Wildlife Library, UK.

The Behavior of Pinnipeds. D. Renouf (Ed.). 1990. Chapman and Hall, London.

The Gray Whale *Eschrichtius robustus.* M.L. Jones, S.L. Swartz & S. Leatherwood. 1984. Academic Press, New York.

The Natural History of Seals. N. Bonner. 1989. Academic Press, London.

The New Encyclopedia of Mammals. D. MacDonald & S. Norris (Eds.) 2001. Oxford University Press, Oxford.**The Northern Fur Seal.** R.L. Gentry. 1998. Princeton University Press, Princeton, USA.

The Pinnipeds: Seals, Sea Lions and Walruses. M. Reidman. 1990. University of California Press, Berkley, USA.

The Sierra Club Handbook of Seals and Sirenians. R.R. Reeves, B.S. Stewart & S. Leatherwood. 1992. Sierra Club, USA.

The Sierra Club Handbook of Whales and Dolphins of the World. S. Leatherwood & R. Reeves. 1998. Sierra Club, USA.

The Whale Watcher's Guide: Whale-Watching Trips in North America. Patricia Corrigan. 1994. NorthWord Press, USA.

Walker's Marine Mammals of the World. R.M. Nowak. 2003. Johns Hopkins University Press, USA.

Whales and Dolphins: Guide to the Biology and Behavior of Cetaceans. M. Wuirtz & N. Repetto. 1998. Swann Hill Press.

Whales and Dolphins of the European Atlantic: The Bay of Biscay and the English Channel. G. Cresswell & D. Walker. 2001. **WILD**Guides Ltd., UK.

Whales and Dolphins—The Ultimate Guide to Marine Mammals. M. Carwardine, E. Hoyt, R. Ewan Fordyce & P. Gill. 1998. Harper Collins.

Whales, Dolphins and Porpoises of the Eastern North Pacific and Adjacent Arctic Waters. A Guide to their Identification. S. Leatherwood, R.R. Reeves, W.F. Perrin & W.E. Evans. 1988. Dover Publications, New York.

Whales, Dolphins and Seals: A Field Guide to the Marine Mammals of the World. H. Shirihai & B Jarrett. 2006. A&C Black, UK.

Whelks to Whales: Coastal Marine Life of Oregon, Washington, British Columbia and Alaska. R.M. Harbo. 1999. Harbour Publishing, Canada.

Photographic credits

Each of the photographs and illustrations used in this book is listed in this section, together with the name of the photographer or artist. Where known, information is included on the location the photograph was taken.

All images by Graeme Cresswell and Dylan Walker courtesy of www.breathtakingwhales.com.

NOTE: North Pacific Right Whale *Eubalaena japonica*: Due to the lack of available images of this species all photographs used are of North Atlantic Right Whale *Eubalaena glacialis*.

Front cover
Pacific White-sided Dolphin *Lagenorhynchus obliquidens*, Peggy Stap.

Introductory sections
TITLE PAGE **Sei Whale** *Balaenoptera borealis*, Falkland Islands, Alan Henry.

What is a marine mammal?
P.11 **Humpback Whale** *Megaptera novaeangliae*: Head, Michael S. Nolan / Wildlife Images.
Common Minke Whale *Balaenoptera acutorostrata*: Head, Ursula Tscherter.
Short-beaked Common Dolphin *Delphinus delphis*: Bay of Biscay, Spain, Hugh Harrop.
California Sea Lion *Zalophus californianus*: Female, Guadalupe Island, Mexico, Phillip Colla / www.OceanLight.com.
Northern Fur Seal *Callorhinus ursinus*: Male, St. Paul, Pribilof Islands, Alaska, Phil Palmer.

Getting started—finding marine mammals
P.12 **Short-finned Pilot Whale** *Globicephala macrorhynchus*: Group logging, Tenerife, Canary Islands, Spain, Dylan Walker.
P.13 **Whale watchers use a GPS**: Dylan Walker.
Whale watchers sight a group of dolphins: Dylan Walker.
P.15 **Watching a Bryde's Whale**: Gran Canaria, Canary Islands, Spain, Dylan Walker.
P.16 **Lighthouse**: Point Reyes, California, Graeme Cresswell.
P.17 **Cirrus clouds**: Seward, Alaska, Graeme Cresswell.
P.18 **Sea states 0–9**: Dylan Walker / Graeme Cresswell.
P.19 **Binoculars**, Dylan Walker.
Spotting scopes: Dylan Walker.
P.21 **Camera equipment**: Graeme Cresswell.

How to identify marine mammals
P.23 **Humpback Whale** *Megaptera novaeangliae*: Unusual V-shaped blow, Bay of Fundy, Nova Scotia, Dylan Walker.
Humpback Whale *Megaptera novaeangliae*: Unusual white individual, Australia, Simon Allen.
P.24 **Baird's Beaked Whale** *Berardius bairdii*: Group with one animal swimming on side, California, Graeme Cresswell.
Short-finned Pilot Whale *Globicephala macrorhynchus*: Bow riding, Tenerife, Canary Islands, Spain, Dylan Walker.
P.25 **Humpback Whale** *Megaptera novaeangliae*: Swimming beside whale-watching boat, Keflavik, Iceland, Dylan Walker.
Humpback Whale *Megaptera novaeangliae* **and Sooty Shearwaters** *Puffinus griseus*: Graeme Cresswell.
P.26 **Sea Otter** *Enhydra lutris*: Monterey, California, Graeme Cresswell.
Humpback Whale *Megaptera novaeangliae*: Breaching, Graeme Cresswell.
Northern Elephant Seal *Mirounga angustirostris*: Bull displaying, California, Dylan Walker.
Long-beaked Common Dolphin *Delphinus capensis*: Baja California, Mexico, Matt Hobbs.

Dorsal fin
P.27 **Sperm Whale** *Physeter macrocephalus*: Hugh Harrop.
Dwarf Sperm Whale *Kogia sima*: East of Abaco, Bahamas, C.D. MacLeod.
Fin Whale *Balaenoptera physalus*: Gulf of St. Lawrence, Ursula Tscherter.
Harbor Porpoise *Phocoena phocoena*: Robin W. Baird.
Pacific White-sided Dolphin *Lagenorhynchus obliquidens*: Peggy Stap.
Risso's Dolphin *Grampus griseus*: Monterey Bay, California, Peggy Stap.
Killer Whale *Orcinus orca*: P.M. Gonzalez.
Fin Whale *Balaenoptera physalus*: Graeme Cresswell.

Coloration and patterning
P.28 **Northern Bottlenose Whale** *Hyperoodon ampullatus*: Isle of Skye, Scotland, Graeme Cresswell / Dylan Walker.
Pacific White-sided Dolphin *Lagenorhynchus obliquidens*: Peggy Stap.
Risso's Dolphin *Grampus griseus*: Steven Hajic.
P.29 **Short-beaked Common Dolphin** *Delphinus delphis*: Porpoising, Bay of Biscay, Spain, Hugh Harrop.
Long-beaked Common Dolphin *Delphinus capensis*: Porpoising, Baja California, Mexico, Thomas Jefferson.
Pantropical Spotted Dolphin *Stenella attenuata*: Porpoising, Ecuador, Stephanie A. Norman.
Striped Dolphin *Stenella coeruleoalba*: Porpoising, Bay of Biscay, Spain, Hugh Harrop.

Number and composition
P.30 **Risso's Dolphins and Pacific White-sided Dolphins** *Grampus griseus* and *Lagenorhynchus obliquidens*: Peggy Stap.

Behavior

P.31 **Killer Whale** *Orcinus orca*: Michael S. Nolan / Wildlife Images.

P.32 **Blue Whale** *Balaenoptera musculus*: Alison Gill.

Blows

P.32 **Blue Whale** *Balaenoptera musculus*: Olasvik, Iceland, Graeme Cresswell.

Fin Whale *Balaenoptera physalus*: Bay of Fundy, Nova Scotia, Graeme Cresswell.

Sei Whale *Balaenoptera borealis*: Doug Perrine / www.SeaPics.com.

Bryde's Whale *Balaenoptera edeni*: Maldives, Charles Anderson.

P.33 **Humpback Whale** *Megaptera novaeangliae*: Keflavik, Iceland, Graeme Cresswell.

Common Minke Whale *Balaenoptera acutorostrata*: Graeme Cresswell.

Gray Whale *Eschrichtius robustus*: Monterey Bay, California, Graeme Cresswell.

North Atlantic Right Whale *Eubalaena glacialis*: Bay of Fundy, Grand Manan Island, New Brunswick, Kristi M. Willis.

Sperm Whale *Physeter macrocephalus*: Kaikoura, New Zealand, Sam Taylor.

Longman's Beaked Whale *Indopacetus pacificus*: Comoro Islands, Olivier Breysse.

Cuvier's Beaked Whale *Ziphius cavirostris*: Cape Hatteras, North Carolina, Graeme Cresswell.

Blainville's Beaked Whale *Mesoplodon densirostris*: East of Abaco, Bahamas, C.D. MacLeod.

Killer Whale *Orcinus orca*: Bering Sea, Alaska, Lori Mazzuca.

Short-finned Pilot Whale *Globicephala macrorhynchus*: Tenerife, Canary Islands, Spain, Dylan Walker.

False Killer Whale *Pseudorca crassidens*: Mercury Bay, New Zealand, Dirk Neumann.

Melon-headed Whale *Peponocephala electra*: East of Abaco, Bahamas, C.D. MacLeod.

Fluking

P.34 **North Atlantic Right Whale** *Eubalaena glacialis*: Cape Cod, Robin W. Baird.

Gray Whale *Eschrichtius robustus*: Monterey Bay, California, Dylan Walker.

Humpback Whale *Megaptera novaeangliae*: Flukes upper side, Graeme Cresswell.

Humpback Whale *Megaptera novaeangliae*: Flukes under side, Peggy Stap.

P.35 **Blue Whale** *Balaenoptera musculus*: Flukes upper side, Ralph Todd.

Blue Whale *Balaenoptera musculus*: Flukes underside, Monterey Bay, California, Peggy Stap.

Sperm Whale *Physeter macrocephalus*: Flukes upper side, Kaikoura, New Zealand, Sam Taylor.

Sperm Whale *Physeter macrocephalus*: Flukes underside, Northern Sea of Cortez, Mexico, Michael S. Nolan / Wildlife Images.

Surfacing sequences

P.36 & P.37 **Common Minke Whale** *Balaenoptera acutorostrata*: Surface sequence 1–3, St. Lawrence River, Quebec, Dylan Walker.

Humpback Whale *Megaptera novaeangliae*: Surface sequence 1–5, Bay of Fundy, Nova Scotia, Dylan Walker.

Sperm Whale *Physeter macrocephalus*: Surface sequence 1–6, Isla San Jose, Sea of Cortez, Mexico, Mark Fischer / AguaSonic.

P.38 & P.39 **Sei Whale** *Balaenoptera borealis*: Surface sequence 1–5, Falkland Islands, Alan Henry.

Bryde's Whale *Balaenoptera edeni*: Surface sequence 1–4, Gran Canaria, Canary Islands, Spain, Graeme Cresswell / Dylan Walker.

Fin Whale *Balaenoptera physalus*: Surface sequence 1–4, St. Lawrence River, Quebec, Dylan Walker.

P.40 & P.41 **Blue Whale** *Balaenoptera musculus*: Surface sequence 1–3: Ursula Tscherter; Surface sequence 4–5: Ralph Todd.

Gray Whale *Eschrichtius robustus*: Surface sequence 1–5, Monterey Bay, California, Dylan Walker.

North Atlantic Right Whale *Eubalaena glacialis*: Surface sequence 1, Bay of Fundy, Grand Manan Island, New Brunswick, Kristi M. Willis; Surface sequence 2–4, Ralph Todd.

Traveling

P.42 **Cuvier's Beaked Whale** *Ziphius cavirostris*: Slow travel, Cape Hatteras, North Carolina, Graeme Cresswell.

Blue Whale *Balaenoptera musculus*: Pair engaged in fast travel, Monterey Bay, California, Peggy Stap.

Fraser's Dolphin *Lagenodelphis hosei*: Group porpoising, Robert L. Pitman / www.SeaPics.com.

P.43 **Risso's Dolphin** *Grampus griseus*: Sharking, Bay of Biscay, Spain, Dylan Walker.

Rough-toothed Dolphin *Steno bredanensis*: Skimming with head and chin clear of the water, Robin W. Baird.

Dall's Porpoise *Phocoenoides dalli*: Rooster tail, San Juan Island, Washington, Stephanie A. Norman.

Risso's Dolphin *Grampus griseus*: Chorus line, Jean Michel Bompar.

Wave riding

P.44 **Common Bottlenose Dolphin** *Tursiops truncatus*: Bow riding, Shark Bay, Western Australia, Jeff Skelton.

P.45 **Pacific White-sided Dolphin** *Lagenorhynchus obliquidens*: Wake riding, Peggy Stap.

Common Bottlenose Dolphin *Tursiops truncatus*: Surf riding, Simon Allen.

Pacific White-sided Dolphin *Lagenorhynchus obliquidens*: Bow riding, Monterey Bay, California, Dylan Walker.

Short-beaked Common Dolphin *Delphinus delphis*: Bow riding, Graeme Cresswell.

Striped Dolphin *Stenella coeruleoalba*: Bow riding, Maldives, Alex Carlisle.

P.46 **Northern Right Whale Dolphin** *Lissodelphis borealis*: Bow riding, Monterey, California, Robin W. Baird.

California Sea Lion (Galapagos subspecies) *Zalophus californianus wollebacki*: Surf riding, David Fleetham.

Dall's Porpoise *Phocoenoides dalli*: Bow riding, San Juan Island, Washington, Stephanie A. Norman.

Melon-headed Whale *Peponocephala electra*: Bow riding, Maldives, Charles Anderson.

False Killer Whale *Pseudorca crassidens*: Bow riding, Maldives, Alex Carlisle.

Resting

P.47 **California Sea Lion** *Zalophus californianus*: Thermoregulating in the water, Monterey Bay, California, Phillip Colla / www.OceanLight.com.

Sea Otter *Enhydra lutris*: Rafting, Simpson Bay, Prince William Sound, Alaska, Heidi C. Pearson.

Harbor Seal *Phoca vitulina*: Hauling out on beach, Frank S. Balthis.

Short-finned Pilot Whale *Globicephala macrorhynchus*: Logging, Tenerife, Canary Islands, Spain, Dylan Walker.

Surface feeding

P.49 **Blue Whale** *Balaenoptera musculus*: Lunge feeding, Sea of Cortez, Baja California Sur, Frank S. Balthis.

North Atlantic Right Whale *Eubalaena glacialis*: Skim feeding, Cape Cod, Massachusetts, Sue Rocca.

Common Minke Whale *Balaenoptera acutorostrata*: Lunge feeding, Ursula Tscherter.

Gray Whale *Eschrichtius robustus*: Skim feeding on krill, Monterey Bay, California, Peggy Stap.

P.50 **Humpback Whale** *Megaptera novaeangliae*: Bubble netting, Michael S. Nolan / Wildlife Images.

Humpback Whale *Megaptera novaeangliae*: Echelon feeding, Michael S. Nolan / Wildlife Images.

Sea Otter *Enhydra lutris*: Tool usage. Stone placed on belly to use as an anvil, Pescadero S.B., California, Frank S. Balthis.

Breaching

P.51 **Killer Whale** *Orcinus orca*: British Columbia, Robin W. Baird.

P.52 **Gray Whale** *Eschrichtius robustus*: Guerrero Negro, Baja California Sur, Mexico, Pádraig Whooley.

Sperm Whale *Physeter macrocephalus*: Northern Sea of Cortez, Mexico, Michael S. Nolan / Wildlife Images.

North Atlantic Right Whale *Eubalaena glacialis*: Cape Cod, Massachusetts, Sue Rocca.

Fin Whale *Balaenoptera physalus*: Stellwagen Bank, Ron Evenden.

P.53 **Humpback Whale** *Megaptera novaeangliae*: Breaching, Peggy Stap.

P.54 **Cuvier's Beaked Whale** *Ziphius cavirostris*: Male breaching, Todd Pusser.

Blainville's Beaked Whale *Mesoplodon densirostris*: Male breaching, Kona coast, Hawaii, Michael S. Nolan / Wildlife Images.

Baird's Beaked Whale *Berardius bairdii*: Breaching, Robert L. Pitman.

False Killer Whale *Pseudorca crassidens*: Mercury Bay, New Zealand, Dirk Neumann.

Dwarf Sperm Whale *Kogia sima*: Breaching, Robert L. Pitman.

P.55 **Striped Dolphin** *Stenella coeruleoalba*: Breaching, Gianni Pavan / CIBRA.

Rough-toothed Dolphin *Steno bredanensis*: Gran Canaria, Canary Islands, Spain, Dylan Walker.

Northern Right Whale Dolphin *Lissodelphis borealis*: California, Graeme Cresswell.

Risso's Dolphin *Grampus griseus*: Offshore San Diego, California, Steven Hajic.

P.56 **Spinner Dolphin** *Stenella longirostris*: Spinning, Oahu, Hawaii, Lori Mazzuca.

Pacific White-sided Dolphin *Lagenorhynchus obliquidens*: Tail-walking, Monterey Bay, California, Peggy Stap.

Pacific White-sided Dolphin *Lagenorhynchus obliquidens*: Somersault, Monterey, California, Robin W. Baird.

Spinner Dolphin *Stenella longirostris*: Somersault, O'ahu, Hawaii, Lori Mazzuca.

Slapping

P.57 **Humpback Whale** *Megaptera novaeangliae*: Pectoral flipper slap, Bay of Fundy, Nova Scotia, Dylan Walker.

Killer Whale *Orcinus orca*: Tail slapping, Donna Hertel.

Killer Whale *Orcinus orca*: Dorsal fin slap, Shetland, Scotland, Dylan Walker.

Humpback Whale *Megaptera novaeangliae*: Head slap, Bay of Fundy, Nova Scotia, Dylan Walker.

Humpback Whale *Megaptera novaeangliae*: Lobtailing, Bay of Fundy, Nova Scotia, Dylan Walker.

Spyhopping

P.58 **Risso's Dolphin** *Grampus griseus*: Spyhopping, Eye Peninsula, Isle of Lewis, Scotland, Alison Gill.

Killer Whale *Orcinus orca*: Spyhopping, Johnstone Strait, British Columbia, Michael S. Nolan / Wildlife Images.

Short-finned Pilot Whale *Globicephala macrorhynchus*: Spyhopping, Maldives, Alex Carlisle.

P.59 **North Atlantic Right Whale** *Eubalaena glacialis*: Spyhopping, Bay of Fundy, New Brunswick, Jeff Skelton.

Common Minke Whale *Balaenoptera acutorostrata*: Spyhopping, Ursula Tscherter.

Sperm Whale *Physeter macrocephalus*: Spyhopping,

Northern Sea of Cortez, Mexico, Michael S. Nolan / Wildlife Images.
Gray Whale *Eschrichtius robustus*: Spyhopping, San Ignacio Lagoon, Baja California, Mexico, Frank S. Balthis.

Other surface maneuvers

P.60 **Humpback Whale** *Megaptera novaeangliae*: Tail throwing, Peggy Stap.
Short-finned Pilot Whale *Globicephala macrorhynchus*: Roll over, Tenerife, Canary Islands, Spain, Dylan Walker.
False Killer Whale *Pseudorca crassidens*: Flipper waving, Maui, Hawaii, Peggy Stap.
P.61 **Risso's Dolphin** *Grampus griseus*: Head-stand, Graeme Cresswell.
Humpback Whale *Megaptera novaeangliae*: Flipper waving, Bay of Fundy, Nova Scotia, Dylan Walker.
Long-beaked Common Dolphin *Delphinus capensis*: Several pods joining to form aggregation, Baja California, Mexico, Robin W. Baird.
Fin Whale *Balaenoptera physalus*: Several individuals aggregating to feed together, Gulf of St. Lawrence, Quebec, Graeme Cresswell.

Breeding

P.62 **Common Bottlenose Dolphin** *Tursiops truncatus*: Two juvenile animals "playing chase," Sea of Abaco, Abaco, Bahamas, C.D. MacLeod.
P.63 **Northern Elephant Seal** *Mirounga angustirostris*: Two bulls fighting for dominance over females, Año Nuevo Island, California, Frank S. Balthis.
Long-beaked Common Dolphin *Delphinus capensis*: Male and female mating, Monterey Bay, California, Peggy Stap.
Northern Elephant Seal *Mirounga angustirostris*: Male and female mating, Monterey Bay, California, Dylan Walker.

Northern Elephant Seal *Mirounga angustirostris*: Mother and nursing pup, Año Nuevo Island, California, Frank S. Balthis.

Inter-pecies associations

P.64 **Common Bottlenose Dolphin and California Sea Lion** *Tursiops truncatus* and *Zalophus californianus*: Association between cetaceans and seals, Guadalupe Island, Mexico, Phillip Colla / www.OceanLight.com.
Fin Whale and Short-beaked Common Dolphin *Balaenoptera physalus* and *Delphinus delphis*: Association between whales and dolphins, Scotian Shelf, Nova Scotia, Sascha Hooker.
Humpback Whale *Megaptera novaeangliae*: Association between Humpback Whale and people, Hervey Bay, Australia, Alex Wilson.
Humpback Whale *Megaptera novaeangliae* **and Sooty Shearwaters** *Puffinus griseus*: Association between cetaceans and birds, Monterey Bay, California, Graeme Cresswell.

Stranding

P.65 **Cuvier's Beaked Whale** *Ziphius cavirostris*: Stranding, Norfolk, England, Graeme Cresswell.

Marine mammal families

P.66 **North Atlantic Right Whale** *Eubalaena glacialis*: Head in profile, Bay of Fundy, New Brunswick, Jeff Skelton.
P.67 **Gray Whale** *Eschrichtius robustus*: Spyhopping, San Ignacio Lagoon, Baja California, Mexico, Michael S. Nolan / Wildlife Images.
P.68 **Fin Whale** *Balaenoptera physalus*: John Young.
Sperm Whale *Physeter macrocephalus*: Back, blowhole and blow, Gianni Pavan / CIBRA.
P.69 **Cuvier's Beaked Whale** *Ziphius cavirostris*: Back and dorsal fin of scarred individual, Bay of Biscay, Spain, Graeme Cresswell.

P.70 **Short-finned Pilot Whale** *Globicephala macrorhynchus*: Blow, head and back in profile, Tenerife, Canary Islands, Spain, Dylan Walker.
Short-beaked Common Dolphin *Delphinus delphis*: Bow riding, Bay of Biscay, Spain, Dylan Walker.
P.71 **Harbor Porpoise** *Phocoena phocoena*: Back and dorsal fin in profile, Bay of Fundy, Nova Scotia, Graeme Cresswell.
California Sea Lion *Zalophus californianus*: Pair swimming, Monterey Bay, California, Dylan Walker.
P.72 **Northern Elephant Seal** *Mirounga angustirostris*: Piedra Blancas, San Simeon, California, Graeme Cresswell.
Sea Otter *Enhydra lutris*: Frank S. Balthis.

Species accounts

P.77 **North Atlantic Right Whale** *Eubalaena glacialis*: *Breaching*, Cape Cod, Massachusetts, Sue Rocca, New Brunswick, Kristi M. Willis; *Head and back in profile*, Regina Asmutis-Silvia; *Head,* Bay of Fundy, New Brunswick, Jeff Skelton; *Head and back showing V-shaped blow*, Ralph Todd; *Tail flukes raised*, Bay of Fundy, New Brunswick, Jeff Skelton; *Blow (inset)*, Bay of Fundy, Grand Manan Island, Jeff Skelton
P.79 **Gray Whale** *Eschrichtius robustus*: *Spyhopping*, Frank S. Balthis; *Back in profile, back and dorsal hump in profile*, Monterey Bay, California, Dylan Walker; *Tail flukes raised, blow (inset)*, Monterey Bay, California, Graeme Cresswell.
P.81 *Calf breaching*, Frank S. Balthis.
P.83 **Humpback Whale** *Megaptera novaeangliae*: *Back and dorsal fin in profile*, Keflavik, Iceland, Dylan Walker; *Mother and calf roll*, Bay of Fundy, Dylan Walker; *Back and blow in profile*, Keflavik, Iceland, Graeme Cresswell; *Spyhopping*, Morten Joergensen; *Tail flukes raised (inset)*, Peggy Stap; *Pectoral flipper, (inset)*, Bay of Fundy, Graeme Cresswell.
P.84 *Fluking*, Peggy Stap.

211

Cresswell; *Back and dorsal fin in profile (inset),* Gibraltar Strait, Spain, T.Walmsley / www. SplashdownDirect.com; *Porpoising,* Jean-Michel Bompar.

P.147 Fraser's Dolphin *Lagenodelphis hosei:* *Group traveling,* Maldives, Charles Anderson; *Pair porpoising, group porpoising,* Robert L. Pitman / www. SeaPics.com.

P.149 Short-beaked Common Dolphin *Delphinus delphis:* *High leap, porpoising,* San Diego, California, Michael S. Nolan / Wildlife Images; *Pair traveling,* Dirk Neumann; *Back and dorsal fin in profile (inset),* Bay of Biscay, Spain, Dylan Walker.

P.151 Long-beaked Common Dolphin *Delphinus capensis:* *Group porpoising, porpoising,* Baja California, Mexico, Thomas Jefferson; *Back in profile (inset),* Peggy Stap.

P.153 Pacific White-sided Dolphin *Lagenorhynchus obliquidens:* *Porpoising,* Michael S. Nolan / Wildlife Images; *Head, back and dorsal fin in profile,* Monterey Bay, California, Graeme Cresswell; *Tail-stand (inset top right),* Monterey Bay, California, Peggy Stap; *Back and dorsal fin in profile (inset bottom left),* Monterey Bay, California, Dylan Walker.

P.155 Northern Right Whale Dolphin *Lissodelphis borealis:* *Pair surfacing, porpoising, (inset top left),* Monterey Bay, California, Peggy Stap; *Porpoising (inset bottom right),* Monterey, California, Robin W. Baird.

P.157 Dall's Porpoise *Phocoenoides dalli:* *Back and dorsal fin in profile,* British Columbia, Robin W. Baird; *Back and dorsal fin in profile, back and*

tail flukes through the water (inset), San Juan Island, Washington, Stephanie A. Norman.

P.159 Harbor Porpoise *Phocoena phocoena:* *Pair showing blow, back and dorsal fin, back and dorsal fin in profile,* Bay of Fundy, Nova Scotia, Graeme Cresswell; *Back and dorsal fin in profile (inset),* Robin W. Baird.

P.161 Vaquita *Phocoena sinus:* *Back in profile, head (inset),* Gulf of California, WWF/ Gustavo Ybarra.

P.165 Northern Fur Seal *Callorhinus ursinus:* *Lone bull lying down, lone bull,* St. Paul, Pribilof Islands, Alaska, Phil Palmer; *Two females,* St. Paul Island, Alaska, Don Getty.

P.167 Guadalupe Fur Seal *Arctocephalus townsendi:* *Bull, mother and pup, swimming with head above water showing large eyes adapted to deep water and night foraging (inset),* Guadalupe Island, Mexico, Phillip Colla / www.OceanLight.com.

P.169 Steller Sea Lion *Eumetopias jubatus:* *Bull and females, group in the water (inset),* Año Nuevo Island, California, Frank S. Balthis.

P.171 California Sea Lion *Zalophus californianus:* *Lone bull,* Frank S. Balthis; *Female with pup,* Guadalupe Island, Mexico, Phillip Colla / www. OceanLight.com; *Pair swimming (inset),* Monterey Bay, California, Dylan Walker.

P.173 Northern Elephant Seal *Mirounga angustirostris:* *Bull,* Big Sur, California, Phillip Colla / www. OceanLight.com; *Weaned pups in the water (inset left),* Año Nuevo Island, California, Frank S. Balthis; *Mother and pup (inset right),* Año Nuevo Island, California, Frank S. Balthis.

P.175 Harbor Seal *Phoca vitulina:* *Adult in the water, (inset),* Marine Mammal Centre, Chris Shields; *Colony,* La Jolla, California, Phillip Colla / www.OceanLight.com.

P.177 Sea Otter *Enhydra lutris:* *Adult resting,* Monterey, California, Graeme Cresswell; *Adult swimming (two images),* Simpson Bay, Prince William Sound, Alaska, Heidi C. Pearson.

Where to go whale-watching in the North American Pacific

Index of common and scientific names

This index includes the common English and scientific names of all the species mentioned in the main text.

Figures in **bold black** text indicate the page on which the main text for the species can be found.

Italicized red figures indicate other page(s) on which a photograph or illustration of the species can be found.

Graeme Cresswell is a conservation advisor, currently working in the United Kingdom with the Environment Team at Norfolk County Council. He has travelled extensively throughout the North American Pacific and North Atlantic where he has now photographed 35 species of marine mammal. He co-authored the **WILD**Guides field guide *The Whales and Dolphins of the European Atlantic*, and has written numerous articles and papers on cetaceans and whale watching. He also works as a tour guide, specialising in trips to California, the Bay of Biscay, and the Canary Islands.

Dylan Walker was travelling onboard a ferry in Scotland when a friendly Minke Whale circled the boat to the delight of everybody onboard. Like many people who have been lucky enough to encounter whales and dolphins in the wild, it was a life-changing experience. Since then, Dylan has dedicated his career to these animals. His focus has been on encouraging other people to share in the wonders of watching and studying cetaceans. Dylan is a co-founder of the marine charity Organisation Cetacea (ORCA), and produces natural history books which support conservation through WILDGuides.

Todd Pusser is a marine biologist and wildlife photographer from North Carolina, USA. For the past 10 years he has traveled the world's oceans documenting little-known cetacean species, spending between six and eight months at sea each year. His photography, which includes rarely seen dolphins and beaked whales, has appeared in calendars, magazines, and books worldwide.